Computer Essays
for Management

Computer Essays
for Management

Jerome Kanter

PRENTICE-HALL, INC. *Englewood Cliffs, New Jersey 07632*

Library of Congress Cataloging-in-Publication Data

Kanter, Jerome.
    Computer essays for management.

    1. Management—Data processing.   2. Information
storage and retrieval systems.   I. Title.
HD30.2.K36   1987   658′.05   86-30651
ISBN 0-13-165994-4

Editorial/production supervision: Colleen Brosnan
Cover design: Lundgren Graphics, Ltd.
Manufacturing buyer: Gordon Osbourne

This edition published 1987 by Prentice-Hall, Inc.
A Division of Simon & Schuster
Englewood Cliffs, New Jersey 07632

Printed in the United States of America

10 9 8 7 6 5 4 3 2 1

ISBN 0-13-165994-4   025

Prentice-Hall International (UK) Limited, *London*
Prentice-Hall of Australia Pty. Limited, *Sydney*
Prentice-Hall Canada Inc., *Toronto*
Prentice-Hall Hispanoamericana, S.A., *Mexico*
Prentice-Hall of India Private Limited, *New Delhi*
Prentice-Hall of Japan, Inc., *Tokyo*
Prentice-Hall of Southeast Asia Pte. Ltd., *Singapore*
Editora Prentice-Hall do Brasil, Ltda., *Rio de Janeiro*

Table of Contents

■

Preface

This book could well be subtitled "Managing *with* Information Systems" to delineate the subject and audience I am addressing, and to distinguish it from the similar-sounding, but quite distinct concept of "management information systems." These essays, aimed at both information systems management and senior functional line and staff management, are designed for a changing information systems world.

Tomorrow's managers, relying less and less on an information systems cadre for support, will be in control themselves. They will use information as a natural extension of their management domain, as a tool not only to support, but to shape their activities. *They* will be the prime force in establishing priorities and allocating resources to information systems projects.

"End user" commonly denotes those who are supported by information systems, as opposed to those who design the systems and produce the output. The term end user may well become an anachronism due to the confluence of roles of the information systems provider and user. A principal objective of this book is to shed more light on the coalescence of the two worlds.

Individual essays are aimed at making tomorrow's business manager aware, in general, of information system trends and, in particular, of the dimensions of the PC revolution; familiar with some specific technologies that will have the most impact; and cognizant of computer literacy needs. This will better prepare the manager to:

■ cope with a changing IS world

■ take full advantage of IS developments

■ apply IS to those critical areas that determine business success

■ assume an appropriate IS leadership role

Organization of the Essays

Essay 1 is a stage-setter that discusses ten prevailing forces in the employment of Information Systems, borrowing some from John Naisbitt's best selling book *Megatrends*. Essay 2 follows with a discussion of one of the megatrends, "Information Systems as a Strategic Tool," expanding on what may be the most significant driving force of all.

Essays 3 and 4 are complementary, with Essay 3 discussing the changing role of the IS executive and Essay 4 focussing on the role of senior management in Information Systems. Since the coalition of these two forces is so vital, it is recommended that both parties read both essays.

Essay 5 discusses personal computing, a force affecting all of us. It is aimed primarily at senior management but the IS executive should read it as well, this time wearing his senior management hat rather than his IS custodian hat.

Essays 6 and 7 discuss the important area of planning, emphasizing the need to integrate IS with corporate plans and senior management thinking. Essay 6 looks at planning more from the IS executive vantage point, while Essay 7 approaches the subject from a top-down perspective.

Essays 8 and 9 have the most specific focus and involve the beginnings of system implementation. Essay 8 discusses IS architecture, which can be considered the cornerstone of a well-planned and directed effort. Essay 9, directed at the assessment of risk, rightfully is both a senior management and IS executive concern.

Essay 10 is related to Essay 1 and looks toward the information systems world in the next 5-year period. It serves as a good checklist of those technologies and developments that will bear watching.

About the Author

Director of Consulting Services, Honeywell Information Systems Division, Jerry Kanter has had over 25 years of experience in the technical and managerial aspects of information systems. He formed his current department for Honeywell because he saw the increasing need for good planning to support the productive use of business systems.

A practitioner, writer, and planner, Jerry devotes himself to educational enterprises both at work and in his outside activities. His book, *Management Information Systems,* Prentice-Hall, 1984, is used as a standard text in many information systems courses. He has published four other books and numerous articles. He has taught courses at Babson College and Northeastern, and lectured at Harvard, Dartmouth, Baylor, Northwestern, as well as at both Oxford and Cambridge Universities in England. Jerry also serves as the Director of Babson College's Information Management Studies, a cooperative effort of business and academia to improve the use of Information Systems. He is a graduate of Harvard College and the Harvard Business School.

Acknowledgements

Versions of some of these essays first appeared in the following publications: Essay 1 in *Information Strategy: The Executive's Journal,* Fall 1985; Essay 4 in the *Journal of Systems Management,* April 1986; Essay 5 in *Infosystems,* September 1985, and Essay 6 in *Infosystems,* June 1982; other sections from *Management Information Systems,* Prentice-Hall, 1984.

In addition, I must thank my secretary, Bessie Koshivas, who has been a partner in many of my publications; Roberta Lewis, for her valuable editorial assistance; and Zelda Sokal, "editor extraordinaire," whose wisdom and ebullience kept this project moving.

Computer Essays
for Management

1. Ten IS Megatrends

■

"Prediction is very difficult, particularly as related to the future." — *Bierce & Ionese*

I've been told that this title will ensure that people will read at least the opening paragraph. So, with a nod to John Naisbitt, author of *Megatrends,*[1] I launch into a discussion of the 10 megatrends (or issues) that I feel business managers and Information System (IS) executives must face in the near future. To arrive at what I consider the pressing industry issues, I have also followed the Naisbitt technique of "content analysis" — surveying the literature and leading IS periodicals, and augmenting this with my consulting visits to leading companies.

While these megatrends are explored individually in today's literature, this article provides an integrated checklist. And a proposition that, if these are indeed the IS megatrends, then IS and senior management should ensure that the necessary resources are being devoted to them.

■

The Megatrends

1. Technological Blitz

2. Corporate/IS Planning

3. Backlog and Systems Obsolescence

4. End-User Computing/Decision-Support Systems

5. The Human Dimension/Education

6. IS as a Strategic Tool

7. The Islands of Micros, Communications, and Office Automation

8. Systems Productivity: Fourth Generation Languages and Packages

9. Security/Backup and Availability

10. Artificial Intelligence: Expert Systems and Robotics

Technological Blitz

Every computer decade has had a form of technological blitz, a torrent of new products and services dumped on the market. The 60's were the era of mainframes, the 70's the era of minis, and the 80's are the era of micros. The micro era, with over 100 companies in the act and many times that number in software and services, is producing a blitz that is causing "option shock." The blitz not only involves micros but terminal, peripheral, and communication products as well. Information systems is an industry facing insurmountable opportunities.

To avoid option shock, IS executives must develop a technology plan based on underlying corporate and IS plans. This plan, sometimes termed a "technology scan," reviews the various technological categories and assesses the potential of each to the enterprise's long-range requirements. While no plan can account for every eventuality, a technology scan establishes priorities and can indicate whether a particular product should be analyzed further. A plan will enable a company to get a bit ahead of the shock wave, knowing in which areas to apply its efforts and energies.

Corporate/IS Planning

Studies have suggested that a corporate and IS plan linkage improves corporate financial results. And while most of the findings are based on common reasoning rather than research data, it appears that it is desirable for IS managers to know what strategic directions are envisioned by the company. While it is difficult to predict the future, it can be quite helpful to explore different scenarios.

Consider the strain the deregulation placed on banking and airline systems geared to the rigidity of regulation. Information systems have been the "limiting" items in implementing the changes. It is obvious that lack of flexibility of information systems can severely retard a company's potential to respond. Knowledge of possible changes can increase the chance that IS can react in a reasonable time frame and set information systems priorities more realistically.

It should be mentioned that, in a growing number of situations, the functions of IS Planning and Corporate Planning are being merged under the IS executive. This leads to a natural linkage of plans.

Backlog and Systems Obsolescence

It's a frustrating predicament: the rising backlog of application requests from an increasingly aware user community comes just as many of the bread-and-butter applications—10 to 15 years old and held together by glue and bailing wire—reach a stage where they are no longer maintainable. It is like most modern highway systems—the roads need repair and expansion and both must be accomplished while maintaining existing traffic loads.

Such a problem exists in many IS shops throughout the country. There are no easy solutions, but senior management's sympathy and understanding are required. A trust/respect level is also necessary to permit the needed redesign of major systems. This requires considerable resources and often a hiatus, or at least a slowing down, of new development. It will test the marketing skills as well as the technical skills of IS management. A systems architecture could be established providing a foundation that is more responsive to end-user demands such that the backlog could be intelligently tackled. However, at the outset, it might require taking a step backward in order to take two steps forward.

End-User Computing/ Decision-Support Systems

Many pundits feel that end-user computing and its management is the number 1 issue facing IS executives. *I* see most end-user computing as a form of decision-support system so I have combined them into a single megatrend. There is no question that "extensibility" is the order of the day; information systems are reaching out and extending their influence into the business office, the corporate office, the board room, and the home. Fueled by media hype, as well as the computing mystique, PC-mania, and mainframe malaise, administrators, professionals, middle managers, and senior executives all want to get into the act.

This is a delicate issue that necessitates straddling the fence between a laissez-faire attitude on one side, and a jealously guarded control/custodian approach on the other. The IS executive no longer can directly manage the burgeoning of spreadsheet computation throughout his organization; however he must not abrogate his corporate responsibility to prevent end users from repeating the proliferation stage that IS has gone through—lack of standards and control, fragmentation of data, redundant data bases, and inability to communicate between programs. The hands-off approach is easiest, but establishing broad policy guidelines as to hardware and software options can smooth the transition to a more integrated environment. Initial spreadsheets and other PC applications can then be viewed as prototype stages leading to this integration of end-user computing with IS host computing.

The Human Dimension/ Education

I have paired these two elements because I feel that education is the key to improving the human dimension in IS. There are two sides to this issue. Internal to IS, the focus is on the need to properly recruit, train, and provide career incentives for IS personnel. The demand for people in the emerging technologies exceeds supply and it is essential to have the proper skills-mix to implement advanced applications. It's no longer a batch, COBOL world. Data base, communication, and end-user language skills and experience are required. Studies have shown that systems analysts and programmers do not mind working hard in relative isolation, if their projects are important and challenging, and they are treated professionally. This often requires a management style different from that employed in other departments of the company. On the user and management side, involvement has become an essential ingredient of successful IS. Studies have shown that systems with heavy user-involvement in specification definition are more successful; yet many companies ignore this. A judicial use of steering committees, user review boards, task groups, and timely management review as part of the system development cycle are extremely important.

Surveys show that less than 1% of the IS personnel budget is spent on education and most shops do not have a well-thought-out education program. Education is usually, at best, a part-time responsibility and its end result is uneven.

The growing significance of the human dimension requires a new look at IS education at all levels—internal IS, end users, and end-user management. Management involvement should be positive; education and understanding are the keys. Intelligent communication between IS and its users is critical—and education is the cornerstone.

IS as a Strategic Tool

Information Systems as a strategic tool has become quite popular in IS thinking. The realization is growing that IS can give a company a major strategic advantage in the competitive marketplace. This trend has been seen as a repositioning, or a transition from "supporting the business" to "being the business." Earlier IS applications focused on non-strategic areas of a business (i.e., the basic monitoring of financial performance, or the billing of customers for products shipped). More recent applications center on such strategic areas as assisting product planners in defining new market niches for their company's products or expanding market share by installing terminals in customers' offices to enable them to place orders directly into their vendor's computer.

New technology is continually opening up new opportunities for deployment of IS for strategic purposes. In the banking industry, electronic funds transfer provides the means for a host of new banking services while in retailing, personal computers and videotex allow customers to shop at home. These are just a few examples.

The point is to recognize the changing roles that technology and IS have in a business and to adopt policies and an organization that recognize the strategic implications of IS. For example, when applications are concentrating on support functions (non-strategic), a high-level IS steering committee and heavy management involvement are not as essential as when the focus is on strategic applications. The first step is to recognize what *is* strategic and, in this regard, Megatrend 2 is pertinent—establishing the linkage between business and IS plans.

The Islands of Micros, Communications, and Office Automation

The importance of this issue was stressed in the Harvard Business Review article entitled "The Information Archipelago".[2] My experience supports its finding that this is one of the key concerns for IS management these days. The three areas are called islands because, in most companies, they have been managed as separate entities, operating outside the control sphere of traditional IS. All three islands are relatively volatile and the logical interconnection of them, forming an archipelago, is a significant challenge. The office of the future, with electronic scheduling, calendaring, and electronic mail is still not well understood; the advent of the personal computer adds another complicating dimension. The issues are organizational as well as technical. This is where both the managerial and technical mettle of IS executives will be tested.

Communications is the delivery vehicle that connects the new technologies of office automation and micros to traditional IS. This is the world of PBXs, LANs, VANs, fiber optics, and satellites. Prominent experts have said that if communications, because of its importance and its enormous cost implications, is not high on the IS priority list, then something is amiss. At the same time, they point out the confusion in the area because the giants, AT&T and IBM, as well as other major vendors, have not really made their future directions known. They indicate it still may be too early to determine the route one should pursue to ensure that the necessary communication linkages can be made without continued major overhaul and architectural redesign. This is the predicament that explains why the archipelego or integration of the islands is so difficult to achieve.

Communications these days means the transmission of data, text, image, and voice and therefore encompasses the existing media of phone, facsimile, electronic mail, and tele/video conferencing. All of this has to be integrated with the various data sources inside and outside the company. The need for integration leads to the questions of where data bases should be located, the responsibility for their upkeep, and their evolution over time. The buzzwords for concerns of this type are networking and distributed data processing.

Systems Productivity: Fourth-Generation Languages and Packages

Every presentation on IS trends shows a chart with time on the X axis and cost on the Y axis. The line entitled electronics cost (processor memory chips and circuitry) proceeds from the upper left-hand corner to the lower right-hand corner while the line entitled people cost goes the reverse way. Electronics cost continues to decline an average of 20% per year while people cost has advanced with inflation, only partially offset by a modest increase in productivity. The obvious conclusion is that a good trade-off would be to use electronics in lieu of people. This issue is directly related to Megatrend 3 and is increasing awareness of tools and techniques to improve systems productivity. Among the tools which improve programmer productivity are computer-aided life cycle development, automated project management aids, and application generators which produce pre-tested coding modules. Fourth-generation languages, employing unstructured or English-oriented language to allow end users to process data and/or generate their own reports are also becoming more prevalent.

Application packages are like "wish fulfillment" for the harried IS executive. If he or she can find a pre-developed, pre-coded program that fits the business situation, employment of internal resources and efforts is avoided. There are examples of successful application package usage, but there are horror stories as well. In the latter cases, the packages don't *quite* fit the business environment and the resultant tailoring causes either serious project cost overruns or the aborting of the entire project. Suffice to say, careful analysis of internal needs and a review of the specific package design and operating specifications are keys to success. Referring back to Megatrend 6, it would appear difficult to use a package in a strategic application area since customizing would appear to be essential in obtaining a competitive edge; however, use of packages in support areas would appear a viable option.

Security/Backup and Availability

Information is increasingly being viewed as a corporate resource, as valuable as the traditional resources of money, material, people, and facilities, although most would agree, more difficult to measure. The information resource should be protected both from physical intrusion (accidents such as operation or program error, hardware failure, flood, or explosion) and willful acts such as fraud and embezzlement. The latter are getting a good deal of attention these days as youthful hackers are obtaining access to proprietary corporate and government data bases. The first priority for handling valuable resources is to protect them; however, few IS shops have a comprehensive security and backup plan. As stories of data base intrusions are reported, pressures are coming from senior management to do something in this area.

The priority given to availability depends on both the cost of an interruption in service and the relative risk of that interruption occurring. The more an information system is embedded in the strategic processes of a company, as indicated in Megatrend 6, the less the company can tolerate interruption. Prolonged downtime in an online reservation, manufacturing or hospital system can be disastrous. Availability has become a critical issue to IS operation, requiring first, the use of a system which has the necessary fault logging, self-diagnosis, and online testing to pinpoint failure or potential failure; and second, the system backup and redundancy in the event of failure. Non-stop and never-fail systems are becoming available for high uptime environments. It is time to make security and availability an important dimension of the planning process.

■

Artificial Intelligence: Expert Systems and Robotics

Artificial Intelligence (AI) can be defined as the development of information systems that can emulate human thinking.

In Expert Systems the computer program carries out the decision logic of an expert (i.e., medical diagnostician, machine troubleshooter, or seismic engineer). Expert Systems are emerging from the laboratory and should be followed carefully by senior management and IS professionals.

In Robotics we see another category of AI. The Robot Institute of America defines a robot as: "A reprogrammable, multifunctional manipulation designed to move material, parts, tools, or specialized devices through variable programmed motions for the performance of a variety of tasks." Currently the application of CAD (Computer-Aided Design) and CAM (Computer-Aided Manufacturing) is dominated by manufacturing firms. Commonly, robots can be viewed as emulating the functions of the human hand—grasping, gripping, lifting, moving, and positioning items; the ability to employ vision systems like bar code reading in a supermarket will extend the application of robotics.

Up to now, CAD/CAM has been a special area of computer application, often not under the responsibility of IS. However, systems presently can link factory operations with office operations so that product movement is recorded in the information data base as it passes through various stages in the manufacturing process. Robotics will also inevitably move into other settings such as warehouses, retail businesses, hospitals and banks. While not today a top-priority issue in all companies, robotics, in its broadest sense, must be understood and tracked for its future implications.

■

Conclusion

So what are these megatrends all about? What is the purpose of listing and discussing them? Here are some suggestions for making this list relevant to your needs. First, determine whether this list fits you and your IS environment or whether you want to add a megatrend or two. Then discuss it with people in the IS world as well as with key executives and management users outside the IS realm. See if they agree or can add anything to the list. Next, establish priorities based on the importance of each item to your business and again review them with IS people and your user population. As the last step, ascertain if resources are being expended in accordance with your priorities. If not, "take stock" and then "take the action" required.

There's no denying it—following Megatrends can take considerable time and resources. But on the positive side, the yield can be Megabenefits.

■

References

1. Naisbitt, John. *Megatrends.* New York: Warner Books, 1982.
2. McFarlan, F. Warren, McKenny, James L., and Pyburn, Philip. "The Information Archipelago— Maps and Bridges." *Harvard Business Review,* May-June 1982.

2. Information Systems As a Strategic Tool

"When a man knows he is to be hanged in a fortnight, it concentrates his mind wonderfully." — *Samuel Johnson*

In IS circles, the tendency to think of Information Systems as a strategic tool is growing. Managers are beginning to realize that IS can give a company a major strategic advantage in the competitive marketplace. This trend sometimes has been called a repositioning or a transition from "supporting the business" to "being the business."

This concept or construct has been described by Jim Cash, Warren McFarlan, and Jim McKenney of the Harvard Business School.[1] It is a straightforward construct which adds a perspective for an IS director. In addition, it can be used as a vehicle for discussing IS strategy and planning with upper management. The terms used are not technical, but business-oriented.

The construct is built on the premise that some IS applications focus on non-strategic areas of a business (e.g., the basic monitoring of financial performance), while other IS applications focus on strategic areas such as assisting product planners in defining new market niches for their company's products.

An IS director and his or her management can benefit from assessing current and planned applications for their strategic content, since certain approaches such as high-level steering committees are vital in a strategic portfolio but of scant value in a non-strategic one, and vice versa. Like similar constructs, this one provides a conceptual window through which to view and understand a specific area of operation.

Determining Company Strategies

The first step is to determine what activities are strategic to a company. Michael Porter[2] has developed three generic strategies that can give a company a competitive edge:

1. Be a low-cost producer.

2. Produce a unique, differentiated product or service.

3. Fill the needs of a specialized market.

It follows that an information system which promotes or assists any of these strategies is, by definition, a strategic information system. An example of the first strategy is Texas Instrument's (TI) goal several years ago to be the low-cost producer of digital watches. At that time, any information system which enhanced this strategy, such as one to automate a TI production line, would be considered strategic.

The second strategy, providing a differentiated product or service, is described by Dr. Charles Wiseman.[3]

"A clinical laboratory competes in a tough, commodity-type business where similarity of service has led to a lack of customer loyalty and frequent price discounting. Doctors send specimens to the labs for processing, and test results are often critical for making diagnoses and determining treatments. The lab has enhanced its customer service by offering to install computer terminals in doctors' offices and hospitals and link them to its lab computer. For a small monthly fee, physicians are able to call up test results at any time."

Finally, an example of filling the needs of a specialized market is the strategy of American Motors which focuses their marketing efforts on the vacation/camping motorist by being the dominant supplier in the 4-wheel drive market with their Jeep line. Information systems which support this strategy (such as a marketing model that more sharply defines buying patterns of potential Jeep consumers) would be considered strategic by American Motors.

When the information system itself becomes the differentiated product or means to penetrate a specialized market, it is also a strategic system. For example, Federal Express has announced a facsimile-based service to deliver letters and reports via telephone line and satellite rather than by sending packages via airplane. In this market, the electronic transfer of words becomes the product.

Using the following type of analysis, existing corporate strategy can be assessed. If the company already has a well-conceived strategic plan, then that becomes the base against which current and planned information systems are measured. A beneficial by-product of this type of exercise is the initiation of that all-important linkage between corporate and IS plans.

■

Strategic Impact of an Applications Portfolio – The Strategic Grid

The first step in assessing the strategic content of an applications portfolio is to develop a listing or inventory of major applications. It is important to maintain the proper detail level so that only the major information systems subsets are included and not every minor program. The listing should normally consist of no more than 40 to 50 systems. The applications should be given generic names instead of internal acronyms to enhance communication with management.

These applications should be plotted against the strategic grid (see Figure 1). If the company is organized into business units or product lines (with separate general management, business strategies, and P&L), the applications should be categorized by these units.

Let's take a look at the grid itself. Batch billing or financial monitoring systems are examples of applications in the Support quadrant. These systems normally do not have an impact on the key strategies of the business as they center on transaction processing at the operational level.

An online airline reservation system is an example of an application in the Factory quadrant. This system is most definitely a strategic tool for an airline and since it is online, any downtime or interruption can be catastrophic. The Factory quadrant implies that the system is mature and no major new developments or enhancements are planned and that it operates as a factory to a manufacturer, turning out the product of the enterprise.

An application portfolio with development emphasis in the Turnaround quadrant indicates that the company is moving toward a strategic focus of its IS function. While current applications are not strategic in nature, future or planned applications most assuredly are.

An IS function with both current and planned applications in the strategic arena falls into the Strategic quadrant.

Figure 1
The Strategic Grid

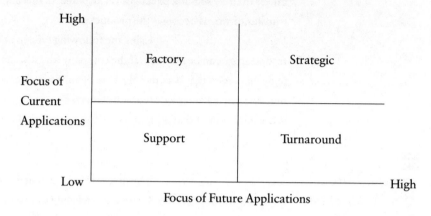

Some generalizations can be made concerning the trend of application portfolios. First, newer technology is opening up opportunities for deployment of IS for strategic purposes. Electronic mail for Federal Express has already been mentioned. In the banking industry, electronic funds transfer provides the vehicle for a host of new banking services while in retailing, personal computers and videotex allow customers to shop at home.

*Application
Portfolio Trends*

Secondly, this type of analysis can highlight differences between senior management's and IS management's view. The strategic grid can be the catalyst in establishing that all-important communication linkage between the two groups.

Finally, the strategic grid analysis can help establish priorities for limited IS resources. It follows that an application that abets a strategic corporate strategy would probably have higher priority than a support application. Also, it may help provide perspective on the extent of the company resources expended on IS. Senior management may be willing to expend more if it is shown that future applications will abet the strategic direction of the corporation.

Procedures Appropriate to Strategic Grid Positioning

Table 1 indicates the activities or procedures that have proven effective for IS application portfolios in the Support or Strategic mode. Normally those applications falling in the Factory quadrant of the strategic grid (Figure 1) would benefit from the procedures listed in the Strategic quadrant because these applications are generally being modified based on changing conditions. However, if the application is a mature one with few if any enhancements, then it functions in a Support mode. In this capacity, driven by an industrial engineering focus, it strives to improve efficiency (in response time, cost control, handling of increasing volumes, etc.) rather than concentrating on effectiveness.

In a review of an application portfolio, anomalies often come to light. For example, it has been found that companies in Support mode application areas often have high-level steering committees and high levels of user interaction. While a modicum of user involvement is useful, management is not overly concerned with Support applications which they feel can properly be the province of the IS staff with limited management review. The specifications are clear and new strategic ground is not being broken. Mismatches of procedures for applications in different quadrants of the strategic grid can be quite counterproductive. Correcting these mismatches can prove most beneficial.

Table 1
Activity/Procedure Matrix

Activity or Procedure	Support	Strategic
Steering Committee	Low	High (Senior Management)
Planning	Low → Medium	High (Link to Corporate)
Risk Profile	Low → Medium	Medium → High
IS Reporting Level	Low	High
User Involvement	Low → Medium	High
Technical Innovation	Low	High
Expense Control Emphasis	High	Low → Medium
IS Director's Managerial Focus	Low → Medium	High
Business Skills Emphasis	Low → Medium	High

Conclusion

The strategic grid approach can provide an improved perspective on IS and can serve as a checklist to ascertain if procedures are consistent with quadrant positioning. In summary, these steps should be followed:

1. Obtain and review corporate strategies or develop them if they are not in written form.

2. Develop an application portfolio listing by business unit.

3. Plot the portfolio against the strategic grid.

4. Review the portfolio analysis with senior management.

5. Resolve differences in positioning between senior management and IS management.

6. Utilize the activity/procedure checklist to determine matches and mismatches.

7. Agree on actions to be taken as a result of the grid/checklist analysis.

Some information systems, though they are supporting strategic directions of the company, have evolved in a random way. An assessment such as suggested here should make these systems more effective. Furthermore, such an assessment could point out new areas where IS can provide the strategic thrust, enabling the company to improve its competitive position. IS as a strategic tool is an idea whose time has come.

References

1. Cash, James, I. Jr., McFarlan, F. Warren, and McKenney, James L. *Corporate Information Systems Management: Text and Cases.* Homewood, IL: Richard D. Irwin Inc., 1983.
2. Porter, Michael E. *Competitive Advantages: Creating and Sustaining Superior Performance.* New York: The Free Press, 1985.
3. Wiseman, Charles. *Strategy and Computers: Information Systems as Competitive Weapons.* Homewood, IL: Dow Jones Irwin, 1985.

3. The Changing Role of the Information Systems Executive

"When you lose sight of your objectives, redouble your efforts."

Clearly there has been an evolutionary shift in the way that IS and the IS executive are viewed within a company. This change is characterized by the progression of titles under which the IS function has operated. In the 50's the department head of IS was called a *computer manager* or *computer center manager.* This implied that the central focus was the computer and that the manager was the custodian of this new electronic device. In the 60's the term data processing came into vogue, and the manager was called the *manager of data processing* or *manager of electronic data processing* (EDP); now the department was called by the function it performed rather than the principal device that performed it. The late 60's brought increasing use of the word *system,* an acknowledgement that an EDP department was comprised of more than a computer and that indeed the principal element being managed was a system. A system consisted of a computer, but also a host of input and output equipment, storage devices, software, applications, and the people that made the whole thing work. The emphasis shifted from the computer to the system.

The 70's ushered in the term *information* as opposed to *data.* Data is defined as raw numbers and files; thus, to be useful to management, data must be processed into meaningful information. The term *information systems* became the preferred descriptor. To this term, the word *management* was then appended, giving us *management information systems* (MIS). Though MIS groups did exist in the 60's, the concept really took hold in the 70's. This addition of the word management was significant, because it indicated a heretofore missing element in the operation. It was becoming apparent that information systems were falling short of their objectives because of a lack of top- and user-management involvement and a lack of management perspective in operating information systems departments. MIS places emphasis on the elements that are the most significant.

The 80's brought a further shift to a new and imposing term—*information resource management* (IRM). *Management* and *information* remain, but *system* has been replaced by *resource*. The concept is that information should be treated as a resource like the more traditional ones of money, material, facilities, and people. MIS, powered by sophisticated computer hardware and software with responsive communication to and from a variety of remote terminals to an integrated data base, has reached the stage where information has become a valuable—or perhaps invaluable—resource in maintaining a competitive business. Whether the head of the IRM function is called an MIS director, an IRM director, or just the CIO (chief information officer), the concept is the same: that of information as a valuable company resource requiring the same plans and controls as for money and materials.

Along with the evolutionary change of the IS title, the role of IS within the organizational hierarchy has been elevated. Starting from a reporting position within the controller's bailiwick, the IS operation now generally reports to the financial or administrative vice-president, to an executive vice-president, or directly to the president.

The title, too, has gradually evolved from Manager to Director to Vice-President. The realization that information is a resource has brought the acknowledgement that its manager should be on the same level as managers of other equivalent resources.

■

Career at the Crossroads

It has been said that the growing demands on the IS executive have created an impossible job description that only a superperson can fulfill.

The evolving nature of the job has added incredible pressures. The IS executive thus finds himself in a challenging, sometimes precarious, position within his company. He must understand the challenge and tackle it effectively in order to survive. The prominent writers on this subject— Withington of A. D. Little, "Coping with Computer Proliferation," Nolan of Nolan, Norton & Company, "Managing the Crisis in Data Processing," and Rockart of MIT, "Critical Success Factors for the Information Systems Executive," have all focused on this topic.

To my thinking, it is a survival issue, with IS executives facing a crucial crossroad of their careers. Since most IS executives have exploited their technical and professional IS skills in arriving where they are, what they need at this point are managerial, organizational, and strategic skills. The user coalitions, often supported by top management, have been waiting in the wings, repressing their hostility; and now they have re-emerged, waving the industry-accepted banner of distributed data processing. It is a bit uncomfortable to be forced away from one's strengths to deal with the opposition on unfamiliar terrain. But that is exactly the challenge for the IS executives. The issues are not technical; they involve strategy, planning, organization, human communication, and leadership.

I was privileged to hear C. P. Snow discuss the two-culture milieu concept in the Godkin lectures he delivered at Harvard in the early 60's. Snow, an Englishman trained in physics with a doctorate from Cambridge, worked in a variety of government agencies; he also was a prolific author, writing more than a dozen novels. He was a "man for many seasons."

Snow's basic concept is that there exists a continued confrontation between the scientist and the humanist. He referred, for example, to the decision on strategic bombing in World War II. The thinking was that bombing a city's population centers would remove the will of the people to resist. This thinking proved to be incorrect. Snow used this issue to show the danger inherent when a prime minister (in this case Winston Churchill) bases a complex technical decision with such far-reaching effects almost completely on a single scientific source (F. A. Lindemann). Snow elaborated on the necessity for the humanist and scientist to reach the proper level of communication and understanding.

The two-culture milieu is most appropriate in discussing the role of the IS executive and the general manager. Often, the IS group develops a culture of its own that is inconsistent with that of the company in which the function resides. This can prove most dangerous, because it is the generalist who must make the final decision. An IS executive, proceeding without management awareness and concurrence, particularly on major strategic issues, can run blindly into disaster. Pursuing a course of innovation and risk-taking in a company that is in a cash bind and a cost-cutting mode, for example, will soon lead to the confrontation suggested above. According to the C. P. Snow philosophy, the outcome will be far from desirable. Successful passage through the career crossroads for IS executives requires a careful balance of the scientific and humanistic worlds.

Information Resource Management

The term *information resource management (IRM)* has already been mentioned. The Diebold Research Program Report (No. 187545) on the Administration of Information Resources states that "The ultimate goal of IRM is to put in place mechanisms (the IRM program itself) to enable the company to acquire or produce the data and information it needs, of sufficient quality, accuracy, and timeliness, and with minimum cost. This is accomplished by creating conditions whereby all levels of the organization come to look upon information not as a free commodity, but rather as a costly and valued asset that must be treated with the same management discipline as is currently afforded financial assets, human resources, material assets and other resources the company utilizes to achieve its aims. In so doing, a major shift from a preoccupation and focus on the power of the technologies, to a focus on the power of the information content, must occur."

The Diebold report goes on to point out the similarities between information as a resource and other corporate assets or resources.

- It possesses fundamental value, as does money, capital goods, labor, or raw materials.

- It has identifiable and measurable characteristics such as method, difficulty, and cost of acquisition; purpose for which used (utility); and different forms and media by which generated, handled, and processed.

- It comes in various degrees of "purity" and utility.

- It must be refined and processed in order to enhance its value.

- It passes through many hands that transport and exchange it from point-of-collection, to point-of-enhancement, to point-of-use.

- Synthetic substitutes are available – some cheaper, some more expensive.

- Information functions can be integrated vertically by buying and processing raw materials. Alternately, costs can be cut by buying processed materials.

- Consumption of the resource can be either expensed or capitalized, depending on management's goals.

- It is an expenditure for which standard costs can be developed and cost accounting techniques employed to help control outlays.

- A cost/benefit equation is possible at each point in collection, handling, enhancement, dissemination, and so forth, which helps manage the efficiency and effectiveness of utilization.

- A variety of deployment choices are available to management in making trade-offs between different "grades," types, and prices.

The report sees the IRM concept and function as important enough to warrant a separate corporate information officer, who would have the responsibility for establishing policies and procedures concerning the information resource. Policies would include a statement of the company's attitude and view of the information it collects, processes, and produces; a procedure to indicate who should have access to different classes of information; the methods of safeguarding and protecting the confidentiality of information against physical disaster, sabotage, or fraud; and an expression of the rights of different groups to information, such as an employee's right to see his own personnel file or a government's right to specific information.

While these issues are real, I do not see the need for a separate information officer or group to oversee this process. I think the IS executive has the responsibility to view information as a resource and incorporate the necessary measures within his operation. Setting up a separate entity in an already complex IS world is, to my way of thinking, counterproductive. IRM is too fundamental a concept and too integral to the operation of IS to be embodied in an outside agency.

■

Scope of Information Resource Management

The concept of IRM broadens the conventional definition of IS. In most companies only a small fraction of the information used throughout a corporation is under the control of IS, at least as IS has been viewed traditionally. Information more broadly conceived includes the letters and memos typed by secretaries, the copying process, telephone service, manuals and catalogs, files and records, and so on. Many firms are using this broader definition to reorganize functions within the company. The thinking is that management of information should not be confined to that portion that is currently in electronic form. The full benefit of integration is not realized unless all information is managed as an entity.

Significant efficiencies can be achieved by optimizing the total flow of information. A simple example should illustrate the point. An executive writes a report, which is typed, edited, corrected, copied, and sent to twenty people within the company. Each recipient has a different time frame in which the information is valid, so each reads and/or files the report for later reference according to his or her need. If the report were produced initially in electronic media, it could be accessed by each executive on a need-to-know basis. When called for, the report could be delivered electronically over a communication line either as hardcopy or as a video display. Teleconferencing, too, could be used to augment the communication process. By integrating and coordinating all the information and its communication, we could make it both more effective and more efficient.

Figure 1 shows the model of an integrated IRM organization that some companies have implemented. A typical IS organization performs the duties in the boxes entitled System Support Services, Planning Controls and Technology, and Processing Services (sometimes not including text processing). Though some IS groups have a few of the information responsibilities listed under Communications and Distribution Services, Reprographics Services, and Records Services, usually these are separate entities managed by other organizations. However, there is much to commend in a plan that places these functions under the IS executive. The concept of IRM broadens the scope of IS and causes a healthy rethinking of what constitutes information and how it should be controlled.

This integration has come to be called the *convergence of technologies*, the technologies being data processing, communication, and office automation. These started as individual islands or entities within a company, often controlled and managed under separate departments. However, there is a strong case for providing bridges or links to connect these islands because they must play an integrated role within the operation of a business. Whether they fall under the same direct management is less important than whether plans, controls, and general management of the functions are integrated by cross-function standards, policy, and strategy.

Figure 1
Integrated Information
Resources Management
Organization

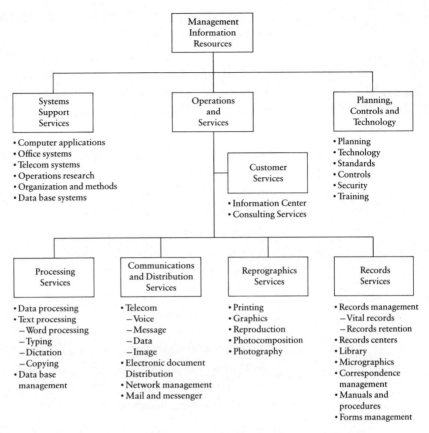

```
                          ┌──────────────┐
                          │ Management   │
                          │ Information  │
                          │ Resources    │
                          └──────────────┘
```

Management Information Resources

Systems Support Services
• Computer applications
• Office systems
• Telecom systems
• Operations research
• Organization and methods
• Data base systems

Operations and Services

Customer Services
• Information Center
• Consulting Services

Planning, Controls and Technology
• Planning
• Technology
• Standards
• Controls
• Security
• Training

Processing Services
• Data processing
• Text processing
  – Word processing
  – Typing
  – Dictation
  – Copying
• Data base management

Communications and Distribution Services
• Telecom
  – Voice
  – Message
  – Data
  – Image
• Electronic document Distribution
• Network management
• Mail and messenger

Reprographics Services
• Printing
• Graphics
• Reproduction
• Photocomposition
• Photography

Records Services
• Records management
  – Vital records
  – Records retention
• Records centers
• Library
• Micrographics
• Correspondence management
• Manuals and procedures
• Forms management

Critical Success Factors for IS Executives

John Rockart, director of MIT's Center for Information System Research, has written extensively about a concept he calls *critical success factors (CSF)*. By analyzing a variety of companies and executives, he has found that a relatively few elements determine whether a particular company or executive will be successful.

Essay 7 will describe the concept of Critical Success Factors (CSFs) as a basis for determining *information system priorities*. CSFs can also be used to determine the key areas of the IS executive's job where high performance is necessary to achieve personal and company goals.

Dr. Rockart[1] interviewed nine directors who, by company and industry standards, were considered highly successful. The objective was to discover those elements or characteristics (CSFs) that appeared to produce success. Synthesis of the data indicates what those IS executives thought was important to them. As I see it, the successful IS executive is generally a business manager, a leader who is aware and concerned with the business, is politically astute in dealing with top management and user management, and recognizes the concepts of information resource management. He is more marketing-oriented than production-oriented and begins to promote IS services through newsletters, annual reports, and the like, taking in general an outward or pro-active approach. Based on Dr. Rockart's study, the following are characteristics of the IS executive.

1. *Customer service*

   - Is perceived as positive by users.

   - Has mechanisms installed to influence perception (user performance index, independent audit, user sign-off, complaint box).

   - Spends increasing amount of time with users.

   - Has charge-out system based on customer-understood and oriented method (charge per transaction or report).

2. *User relations/communications*

   - Knows customers, their CSFs, corporate political leanings, etc.

   - Allows user/top-management involvement in setting application priorities.

   - Is viewed as a leader.

   - Develops clear, concise user interfaces and responsibilities.

3. *People resource*

   - Ensures maximum utilization of this high-quality component.

- Pays attention to career development and training

- Emphasizes management/business focus.

- Interchanges people with line departments.

- Controls turnover.

4. *Repositioning of IS*

- Reports to president or key senior executive.

- Views self as a manager versus a technician.

- Sees a constantly evolving structure; more responsibility to users.

- Focuses on effectiveness versus efficiency.

■

A Business Within
A Business

The classical view of activities within a business, as described by Robert N. Anthony,[2] conform to a triangle with layers of operational control, management control, and strategic planning.

Figure 2
Business Activities

Using this focus to describe the IS function, the *operational control* activities cover the gathering of input, the processing of data through the computer shop, and the production of output in the form of reports or terminal display screens. This level of activity is quite similar to a factory operation within a manufacturing company.

Operators key in data, load and unload tapes and disks, and monitor the activity much like production foremen. In carrying out these functions, the IS operation, like the business it supports, utilizes the resources of money, people, facilities, material, and information. It is enlightening to realize that IS is a user as well as a provider of its own services. It is also enlightening to realize that the "shoemaker's children" syndrome holds true: IS does not often produce information to optimally manage itself.

Management control activities include scheduling computer operations, monitoring hardware utilization, reviewing performance and costs, and managing application development projects. *Strategic planning* involves the development of an IS mission or direction statement as well as a long-range plan to project future hardware, software, application, and people resource requirements.

Thus it is true, the IS is literally a business within a business, operating as a microcosm of the company it supports. This perspective establishes the importance of the IS executive as a business manager using information to control his or her own operation as well as providing information to support the business in general.

■
Conclusion

The job of the IS executive is changing dramatically. The role had been as a technical, inward-looking custodian of computer hardware. The concept of information systems as a strategic tool, the emergence of end-user and personal computing, and the realization that information is a valuable corporate asset, all have changed the old image. This has necessitated a complete re-evaluation of the characteristics and capabilities required to succeed in the IS executive's position.

Improving the situation requires patience and understanding of both the IS executive and top management. The IS executive must recognize the changes, then learn and practice the new skills required to adapt. The senior manager must support the IS executive through proper involvement and top-level leadership. It's a situation that must be faced head-on; it's a top priority issue.

■
References

1. Rockart, John. "The Changing Role of the Information Systems Executive." Center for Information Systems Research, MIT Sloan School of Management, Cambridge, MA, April 1982.
2. Anthony, Robert N. "Planning and Control Systems: A Framework for Analysis." Division of Research, Harvard University, Boston, MA 1965.

4. The Role of Senior Management in IS

■

*"Our organization chart changes so often, it has come to be known
as the chart du jour."*

The use of information systems in the business world will change dramatically in the next ten years.

■ Large companies will organize into small operating units to encourage and benefit from the entrepreneurial spirit created; information systems will respond accordingly.

■ Information systems technology will be embodied in the fabric of business, rather than being considered an adjunct or separate body of knowledge, the domain of the "IS Experts"; functional business managers will manage their own information resources.

■ Information will be viewed as a valuable competitive resource such that application programs and data bases will be carried on the balance sheet and depreciated as corporate assets.

■ Companies will develop competitive advantages by using information systems in ways previously not considered in the realm of IS. Information will begin to shape, as well as support, the business.

■ Companies will implement information systems architectures that integrate office systems, production systems, and decision-support systems with a unified communications network.

■ The true executive workstation will evolve, integrating voice and data, personal and company data, and administrative support with decision-support systems.

These changes both excite and worry the senior management of business enterprises. They excite because information systems offer another way to establish strategic product and market uniqueness. Numerous examples exist of how information systems have provided the competitive edge for business success. At the same time, senior managers worry lest their lack of knowledge of the new technology gives others opportunities for inroads into their markets. What are the information issues with which they should be concerned? The following study will serve to develop those issues, beginning with the IS viewpoint.

The IS Executive View

IS executives from corporations and institutions throughout the U.S. attended a seminar entitled "Planning for Better Use of Information Systems" and, during 1984 and 1985, 80 attendees representing four such seminars recorded their attitudes on 15 preselected issues (see Table 1). The issues were chosen based on research conducted by the Diebold Research Group and the Society for Information Management. I think there would be common agreement that all these issues are relatively high on IS agendas these days.

Table 1

Issues of Importance to IS Executives

Issue	Gap Times Importance	Import-ance	Perform-ance	Gap
1 Linkage of IS/Corporate Plans	11.63	5.50	3.38	2.12
2 Communications with Senior Mgt	9.84	5.95	4.29	1.65
3 Long-Range IS Plan	9.75	5.53	3.77	1.76
4 Education for End Users/Mgt	8.49	5.23	3.60	1.62
5 Security Backup	8.18	5.35	3.82	1.53
6 Telecommunications	7.84	5.71	4.34	1.37
7 Decision-Support Systems	7.01	4.73	3.25	1.48
8 Application Priority Process	6.19	5.21	4.03	1.19
9 Office Automation Systems	5.45	4.81	3.68	1.13
10 Education for IS Personnel	5.23	5.24	4.24	1.00
11 Skills Mix of IS Personnel	4.76	5.23	4.32	0.91
12 Steering Committees	4.41	4.56	3.59	0.97
13 Application Packages	4.31	4.82	3.92	0.90
14 Personal Computing	2.84	4.63	4.02	0.61
15 IS Charge-Out	2.10	4.11	3.60	0.51

Methodology

Each IS executive rated the 15 issues listed as to relative importance on a scale of 1 to 7 as follows:

```
1 - - - - - - 2 - - - - - - 3 - - - - - - 4 - - - - - - 5 - - - - - - 6 - - - - - - 7
```

irrelevant   possibly   important   very

useful   critical

They then were asked to rate their performance on each issue on a scale of 1 to 7 as follows:

```
1 - - - - - - 2 - - - - - - 3 - - - - - - 4 - - - - - - 5 - - - - - - 6 - - - - - - 7
```

very   inadequate   good   excellent

poor

Average importance and average performance were recorded (columns 2 and 3) and a gap between the two was calculated (column 4). This gap is a measure of the seriousness of a particular issue as viewed by IS executives. The gap was then weighted by multiplying it by the importance of the issue and sorted in descending order (column 1).

Conclusions of the Study

The top three issues focus on the importance of IS planning that ties to corporate business plans and the increasing need for IS executives to communicate with senior management. These issues can be critical and, in fact, are so rated in most current surveys or research studies. IS issues seem to be focused outward, toward senior and functional management and the integration of business and IS plans, rather than inward to issues of budgets, internal procedures, techniques for improving efficiency, and the like.

Education, representing only 1-2% of IS budgets, is rated high on the list of critical issues. The issue is end-user management education which is ranked 4th as compared with education of IS personnel which is ranked 10th. This is consistent with the strong attention that is being given to end-user computing and the development of information centers (separate units to provide consulting and support so that end users can access data directly and produce management reports and analyses). The software to provide decision-support systems, ranked 7th, is usually a major part of an information center's capabilities.

It is surprising to see personal computing so low on the list. It may be that the PC impact is more evolutionary than revolutionary, as some have predicted, or it may be that IS executives feel the area is under control. Steering committees, in my opinion, are low on the list because many have just not been effective—a result of the wrong composition and/or the wrong agenda. Yet, I remain convinced that an effective executive steering committee is very important as a vehicle for improving communications with senior management and linking business and IS plans.

This list presents the IS view of crucial issues, but it is a statement to senior management as well, because many of the crucial issues (the top of the list) cannot be improved unilaterally—they demand management involvement. This leads to the view from a senior management perspective.

The Senior Management View

It is becoming increasingly clear that a better informed and involved senior management team can vastly improve the effectiveness of information systems. The information systems profession is a relatively new discipline; the industry is characterized by volatile changes that have been difficult for industry professionals to comprehend and next-to-impossible for non-professionals, senior management included.

Figure 1 illustrates the organizational elements that must be in harmony for effective information systems. This confluence assumes increased significance as information systems focus on management needs as opposed to operational needs.

Figure 1
Organizational
Elements

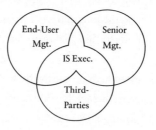

The IS executive deals directly with third-parties (a variety of hardware, software, and support service vendors), but the relationships with end-user managers and senior management must be a cooperative coalition if a company is to fully exploit its information resource.

In my experience, senior management has some or all of the following concerns about information systems.

- Is the technology running away with us?

- Are we spending too much or too little?

- What return on investment are we getting or should we be getting?

- How should we measure the return?

- Is my IS director qualified to monitor the technology to best support the company?

- How does our IS function compare to our competition?

- Do we have a comprehensive long-range direction and strategy?

- Are we treating information as a resource?

- Do our senior managers use information systems?

- Can I use information systems to greater strategic advantage?

- What should be my knowledge/involvement-level?

- Am I part of the problem or part of the solution?

The CEO and senior management are generally thought to be less informed about the IS function than about any other major function in the business. If, indeed, information is viewed as a resource—as valuable or more so than the other resources of the business (cash, inventory, people and facilities)—then there is solid rationale for increased understanding and involvement.

Without such an understanding, the situation is most precarious. Turnover has accelerated in the IS profession with tenure in this high-burn-out area 3 to 4 years or less. This is not a healthy situation. Top management more and more is filling the job with proven managers rather than proven technicians. While there is much to be done on the part of IS executives to improve the perception of their service, the CEO must also play a major role, by first achieving a better understanding of the IS function and then securing the top-office involvement and the backing and support of the IS executive.

The Payoff from Top Management Involvement

There is a lack of solid research into the correlation of top-management involvement and IS success, though conventional wisdom certainly supports this. It is for this reason that I was impressed with research conducted by Professor William J. Doll.[1]

Doll studied 33 firms and characterized them as having successful or unsuccessful IS by a 6-criteria, 37-question set aimed at the results of application development. A high value was placed on completing projects that met design and benefit objectives, were delivered on time and within budget, were adaptable to changing management needs, and were developed in a rational sequence based on expected payoff and probability of success.

Then both IS executives and CEOs were interviewed using a structured question set. As seen in Table 2, it was found that in firms with successful IS, top management made more effective use of four processes.

Table 2
Correlation of
IS Success with
Employment of
Specific Manage-
ment Processes

	"Yes" Answers (%)	
	Firms with Unsuccessful IS Development	*Firms with Successful IS Development*
Executive Steering Committee		
Do you have a systems policy committee, comprised of managers from functional areas of the organization, involved in setting priorities and/or allocating resources for systems development?	23.1	55.0
Written Plans		
Do you have a written overall plan for systems development which (1) covers all major functional areas of the business, and (2) clarifies interrelationships between applications (systems)?	23.1	60.0
Development Priorities		
Do you and higher-level management have a mutually agreed upon set of criteria for deciding which applications (systems) to implement first?	46.2	90.0
Funding Commitment		
Has top management made a long-term commitment to provide stable funding for system development activity?	38.5	70.0

Though Doll is quick to note that the sample is small and the results therefore tentative, the conclusions suggest significant guidelines for both IS executives and top management which appear consistent with successful IS development activities. The proper level of management involvement is not just another way to consume valuable management time; it "pays off," as the successful IS departments in this study illustrate.

Degree of Top Management Involvement

I have conversed with CEOs of large companies who, after we had established rapport, stated that people were preaching to them all the time about their involvement in IS. Publications and seminars hammer home the theme that information and its management have become both critical and strategic. But the CEO asks, "*How* and *where* should I get involved? I have to pick the shots carefully because I'm already putting in 12 hours a day and I don't see too many things dropping off my agenda."

As a "starter kit" for this process, the following matrix (Figure 2) is presented. A variety of activities associated with the IS function are listed while four gradations of CEO involvement are indicated. Level 1 activities are so important to the business that the CEO should personally *approve* the activity. Level 2 activities are those that the CEO should *insist* that his company do, though it may or may not be necessary for him to approve the activity itself.

Figure 2
CEO Involvement/
Responsibility
Matrix

	Activity	Level 1 Approve	Level 2 Insist	Level 3 Review	Level 4 Delegate
1.	Long-Range IS Plan	X	X		
2.	Application Portfolio Determination			X	
3.	CEO Decision-Support System Specification	X			
4.	IS Budget and Resource Allocation			X	
5.	Security/Backup Plan		X		
6.	IS Mission Statement		X		
7.	Selection of IS Executive			X	
8.	Technological Risk Assessment	X	X		
9.	Design of Systems				X
10.	Hardware/Software Selection				X

(table header: CEO Levels of Involvement)

Level 3 activities should be reviewed by the CEO though they need not personally be approved. Finally, Level 4 activities are those that should be *delegated,* usually to the IS executive or to user management. It is felt that this type of thinking can begin to build the business partnership between the CEO and IS executive that is so vital to effective information systems.

Referring to Figure 2, the CEO should insist that an IS long-range plan exists; furthermore, he should approve it, and should ensure that it is consistent with corporate strategies. This is probably the most significant area for CEO involvement; yet it is far from an accepted practice.

It would seem that a prioritization process for directing information resources to different functional areas of the business is necessary. For the most part, the CEO should not be asked to approve either the process or the resulting application portfolio. However, the CEO should review and have influence in key projects that have a far reaching effect on the company. Certainly a new reservation system for an airline, an online ordering system for a distributor that links customers with the data base, or the entry of a financial institution into electronic cash transfer are applications worthy of the CEO's involvement. At a minimum, the interest of the CEO will impress the implementers with the importance of the project, and ideally, allow the CEO to add his perspective to the overall direction of the application. The application areas under question are large, complex ones usually involving multi-man-years of effort.

Certainly, for an executive decision-support system that he will personally use, the CEO must demand final approval. Survey results of decision-support systems, conducted by the Society for Information Management support the idea that those systems which executives initiated and were heavily involved in were the most successful; yet such involvement occurred in only 12 of the 56 systems studied.

IS budgets should have CEO review. It would be unfortunate, because of an overemphasis on cost-containment, to overlook applications that offer strategic advantages. A balanced approach is needed. Since it may be prudent to allow the IS operation to grow at a rate faster than other operations, the CEO perspective may be a necessity.

As has been mentioned, with so much dependent upon information systems and the information itself, information resources and assets must be protected. The CEO, while not needing to approve, should insist there is a formal plan and program in place for information backup and security.

A mission statement, outlining the strategic direction of IS within the company, is a vital but often missing element. This statement is the charter upon which the IS long-range plan is based. As with a security plan, the CEO should insist there is such a charter though he or she need not approve it.

The selection of an IS executive is both crucial and sensitive. If the incumbent reports directly to the CEO, then obviously he should have the final decision, but even if he reports through an Executive VP, Administrative VP, or Controller, the selection should be reviewed by the CEO. The incumbent should know that he or she is there with the full cognizance and approval of the CEO. The position is so important that the confidence and respect of the top officer is essential for success.

With rapid changes in technology, it is important for the IS executive to know the company's propensity for risk, that is, whether the strategy should be a "following" one rather than a "pioneering" one or somewhere in between. For example, employing leading-edge satellite communications is an expensive proposition with fairly high risk but with considerable benefit once implemented. This type of decision warrants the direct involvement and approval of the CEO. He must also insist that his views are known on this matter.

There are obviously many matters in which the CEO should not be involved. For example, the design of systems and hardware/software selection should be handled by professionals using state-of-the-art methodologies.

This matrix is not an all-inclusive list, but it does indicate important areas of executive concern. More important it is meant to make the CEO pause to reflect about his personal IS-involvement level. A CEO must consider many functions; this section should encourage more personal involvement in a discipline that begs for direction and guidance. The question should be asked, "Am I part of the problem or part of the solution?"

Common CEO/IS Perspectives

The CEO/IS partnership is obviously dependent on actions on both sides. There are approaches the IS executive must take to facilitate the CEO's interest and involvement in information systems. The salient point is that he must act more as a businessman than a technician and, with this in mind, the IS executive must follow the guidelines described, and the CEO should *insist* on them as well.

Establish Consistent Performance and Work Criteria for IS

IS should be measured by the same criteria that are used throughout the business. If the organization utilizes MBO (management by objective) or has a particular results-orientation, those same principles should be applied to IS. The same return on investment or profit standards should be applied. Cost accounting reports and other management reports should be employed for IS as for other areas of the operations. As the IS department begins to adopt the procedures of the company, so should the individuals. Accounting for time spent on jobs and efforts to measure productivity should be incorporated. More and more, the IS department's mode of operation should be consistent with the rest of the organization. The procedures should be applied fairly and uniformly to avoid a counter-reaction from the IS people. These measures should be instituted in such a way that the individuals regard them as an aid in better managing their time and activity and not as a bridle to their innovation and creativity.

Consider the Basic Computer Feasibility Criteria

It is important not to attack the wrong management problems and attempt to computerize an activity that just isn't a feasible IS application. There are seven computer feasibility criteria, most of which, I feel, are necessary to make computerization worthwhile:

- high volume of transactions
- repetitive nature of transactions
- reasonable amount of mathematical processing
- necessity for quick turnaround
- accuracy and validity of data
- common source documents
- well-understood processing logic

I believe that these criteria apply to management-oriented applications as well. One-time functions that involve a good deal of programming and data-gathering are not feasible applications. It is better that problems surface at the outset than to continue to pursue a "will-o'-the-wisp" application with only a marginal return possible. If an unproductive application is rejected, credibility will be established, paving the way for acceptance of management applications with real payoffs.

Maintain Simplicity

I have always liked the phrase "elegance in simplicity" and am convinced that the most effective computer applications are those that are straightforward, easy to understand, and easy to operate. Systems analysts will have better success working with management if they talk about simplifying the analysis or the data that the manager must review. The "information-overload syndrome" is still prevalent today. Business operations have grown in volume and complexity; a good systems analyst can help cut through this complexity, eliminate the extraneous, combine two reports into one, and eliminate other data completely. We still "kill too many fleas with elephant hammers."

In my visits to computer departments and in discussions with managers, I often wonder what happened to the "management-by-exception" principle. No wonder paper costs have risen; our high-speed printers and copying machines turn it out by the ton, with no relief in sight. I am firmly convinced that IS can favorably impact management if it can demonstrate how to streamline the decision process and simplify the underlying data that supports the decision. I like the apology appended by a professor to a very long letter sent to a colleague, "I would have written a shorter letter, but I didn't have the time." It takes effort to be concise and meaningful—but the effort should be made. Business, government, and life in general, have become complex enough; we should employ information systems to simplify rather than add to the complexity and confusion. Thus, a plea at this stage is for elegance in simplicity.

Train Systems/ Business Analysts

Obviously a prerequisite to accomplishing any job is competent people. So it is with IS. More and more, the major qualification of successful systems people is a solid business perspective. The technical side of the job is important — the *how* something gets done — but the *what* is even more important. It is the *what* dimension that IS people have in common with non-IS managers; this should be the starting point for closer cooperation and communication.

To develop systems that aid management, we need a new breed of systems people who are business-oriented first and IS-oriented second. Schools and universities must help in the training process; I have long felt that institutions stress the technical side of computers and give inadequate attention to the relationship of information to the management process and how computers influence this process.

This new breed was called "Renaissance People" in a talk by Dean Donald C. Carroll. He pointed out that information technologists who don't understand management problems often err by developing elegant solutions to non-problems. The "Renaissance People" would combine technical expertise with the management function and organization.

We must understand that the control of business and business decisions is not in the hands of specialists; it is in the hands of business generalists. The IS professional must fully comprehend this basic truth and direct his or her intellect and expertise toward aiding the generalist in making better decisions — remembering that the decisions and the manner in which they are made are the province of management.

One of the healthiest situations has been the interchange of people within the IS and operating areas of a company. It makes good sense to staff the IS department with personnel from operating departments who show an aptitude and an interest for systems work. Similarly, system analysts should receive a "tour of duty" outside of IS, in order to appreciate the problems of the actual business world and understand the difficulties of putting an advanced new system into productive operation.

Whenever possible, IS and operating personnel should be assimilated in everyday business activities. At conferences, work sessions, or business functions, the groups should be encouraged to work together, to take every opportunity to discuss and explore things together. If possible, IS people and operating people should travel together, engage in social activities together, and develop an awareness of each other's view on business matters. Most people are prone to stay with employees of their own department and to discuss matters with people of similar background. This situation does nothing to facilitate the understanding and resolution of problems; it merely reinforces one's predetermined judgment on the matter. And finally, there is the opportunity to work together on special projects that require inter-disciplinary participation. Mutual confidence and respect are built up when a task is accomplished by such a group.

Conclusion

The business environment in the information age will not continue to be "they" (IS people) and "us" (business people). Along with the recognition of information as a resource, will come the realization that company data belongs to the managers of that company rather than to its information systems people. The latter are the custodians of the data, not its owners. This places an added burden on both the IS executive and the top executive of a company. It necessitates a rethinking of roles and responsibilities and a changing managerial style—changes highlighted in the responsibility matrix. What worked yesterday will not work today; IS technology has created an entirely new management environment.

Even though it is very difficult to change a behavioral pattern that is deep-rooted and has proven successful in the past, such a change is exactly what is required on the part of the CEO and the IS executive.

The IS executive must turn outward to the CEO and to senior management to form the coalition that is so important to his success. In doing so, he must call upon skills not needed previously or which may have atrophied, if there at one time. These attributes are managerial and marketing; both are needed to communicate with and gain the proper involvement of senior management.

At the same time, the CEO must get involved and give top-level direction to a function he has almost completely delegated in the past to the IS executive. This is vital to an effective IS operation. The CEO/IS partnership is needed to build the team management style that will become the key ingredient in "managing with information systems."

Reference

1. Doll, William J. "Avenues for Top Management Involvement in Successful MIS Development." *MIS Quarterly,* Society for Information Management and University of Minnesota. March 1985.

5. Practical Considerations in Personal Computing

■

"The only difference between men and boys is the price of their toys."

"Everyone is giving me advice on why I should use a Personal Computer. I receive all kinds of signals; some subtle, others not so subtle. When I travel, I count more than a dozen ads in every airline magazine relating how this box can free me from mundane administrative tasks while that box can help me make better decisions. My IS director wants me to attend a seminar on management uses of information. I see an increasing number of requisitions from my operating managers for PCs. I note a Charlie Chaplin character and an assortment of fruit (Macintoshes and the like) beamed at me between plays of the Super Bowl. There is a superabundance of technology promising to improve my business and professional life. Are they trying to tell me something?…"

The above describes the feelings of a manager who will be referred to later in this essay as a "struggler." It is a stage-setter for the discussion of four types of management users of personal computers. I will begin by briefly reviewing the trends in personal computing, drawing from various studies and my own experience. Then I will categorize management users of Personal Computers, because treating them as a homogeneous group can be extremely misleading. Based on this categorization, I will present an end-user manager manifesto, indicating six areas where actions can improve personal computing effectiveness. The manifesto views the world from the manager's perspective, a perspective based on published research, my own experience as a management user of Personal Computers, and that of many managers with whom I have consulted, both on and off the record.

It is the off-the-record experience upon which I place the most weight, since some managers answer questionnaires or respond to live questions with a bit of a "halo effect"; they become ecstatic if their latest spreadsheet lines up with all the numbers in columns, regardless of whether the data and formulas are correct and regardless of the time and energy it took to produce the results. Thus, their stated views are much more positive than their experience as expressed off the record.

■

From Clutter to Integration

It was reported several years ago that, for a specific period, books on computers and technology outsold books on sex and physical fitness. While this may be a fleeting phenomenon, computer literature *is* proliferating, with the leading subjects being "End-User Computing" and the "Role of the Personal Computer." Numerous published articles and research studies which focus on these subjects have the following common themes:

- End users can be categorized as 1) managers, 2) professionals, 3) administrators, and 4) clerical. There is far greater user saturation in the latter three categories than at the manager level.

- There is little, if any, interaction with the central data source and most data is keyed in by the user.

- When one considers the personal time of application and data preparation, the cost per application can reach $20,000 or more. There is limited cost-justification, as in most cases the benefits are intangible but obvious.

- The term "user-friendly" is a euphemism if the user is defined as a manager; a better term would be "user-accessible."

- There are few, if any, controls or procedures for personal computing applications; for example, floppy disks often are not copied to provide backup in case of accidental destruction nor are security measures followed to protect proprietary data.

These surveys reveal a condition called "techno-logical clutter." A manager may have a "smart" telephone with memory to hold frequently used numbers, time calls, etc., and in addition, have a Personal Computer in his office. His secretary has a different type of PC for word processing and electronic mail and his administrative assistant may use a terminal or yet another make of PC to tap the central data base or an outside time sharing service. The technology is far from integrated.

Most studies project a future where the Personal Computer will be as common as the telephone and will be called an Executive Workstation (EWS). The EWS would keep track of engagements, meetings, schedules, significant data on business contacts; provide for decision support, where necessary accessing the central data base; and facilitate electronic message storage and forwarding. The EWS would be compatible with other departmental workstations. The time frame needed for the transition from "clutter" to "integration," however, is quite uncertain.

Four Kinds of Management Users

Management users, and would-be management users, can be thought of in four categories: (1) The Open Cynic, (2) The Hidden Cynic, (3) The Techno-Type, and (4) The Struggler. These categories are based on real people who have presented their views at meetings, in private consultation, or in writing.

The Open Cynic

The open cynic is a manager strong enough or high enough in the organization to state a view which may be considered a bit anachronistic by his peers. The open cynic feels that the Personal Computer is far overrated and does not belong on an executive desk. The executive or manager must know what data is available and what spreadsheets and decision-support can do, but using them can be delegated to financial or administrative support people. Manipulating spreadsheets or doing word processing is the work of a financial analyst or secretary, not the function of a manager. A manager's main job is to develop conceptual plans and measurable goals for a specific functional area of the business and to motivate and direct the people under him to achieve the prescribed goals, thereby accomplishing the plan. The open cynics will point out that a relatively small portion of their job deals with numbers; the majority of time is spent on concepts, people, and things. Here are actual statements made by important high-level executives of major companies; the sentiments are shared by many more.

- A senior manager of a bank referred to the computer as modern man's Lionel Train. He said, "They're fun to run and to give you that personal sense of control, but they can't accomplish much for you in the way of management work." He went on to say that the costs are deceptive. Individually, they're inexpensive, but when you multiply by 100 or so, you've got a significant investment, and he added that he has hundreds of micros scattered around his organization.

- An insurance executive expressed concern that his people were "spending too much time programming their micros" – developing the formulas in Lotus 1-2-3 and inputting the data manipulated by the formulas. He added that he pays his managers to supervise people, review strategies, and carry them out, not to become computer jocks. "It's not so much the cost of the equipment, it's the loss of productivity of high-priced managers and professionals not doing the job they're getting paid to do." He emphasized that he could hire programmers to develop and exercise spreadsheets.

- A president of a medium-sized manufacturing company expressed it this way: "It takes our Group VP three days to do his tax return compared to one day previously. Office automation is highly overrated – rather than send an electronic message, it's better to go down the hall and talk to someone. Everyone's trying to sell me a terminal or a Personal Computer. We don't need to be online and I don't need the information instantly – all we need to run our business is the ability to track key indicators on a board: bookings, profit, inventory, expenses, etc. That's how I manage – why would I want or need this information 'online'? Computers complicate things – they make mountains out of molehills."

The Hidden Cynic

This type of manager may present more problems than the open cynic. The hidden cynic feels the same about managerial use of PCs, but is not strongly enough positioned to state his real feelings; he feels that an unenthusiastic view on PCs is not consistent with the image of the modern executive. Hidden cynics can be found after business hours when, over dinner, they relax and tell you what they really feel. What's disconcerting in their case is that they often get swept along with the tide, mislead IS people, and wind up with a good deal of hardware in and around their offices which doesn't get used. The hidden cynic may show a brief flurry of enthusiasm and begin learning spreadsheet manipulation, but this soon dies down as the exigencies of his job take hold.

In organizations, peer and power pressures determine the existence of open and hidden cynics. If the boss is an open cynic, the lower-level cynics can come "out of the closet" and declare themselves. If the boss is a hidden cynic because of a sense of technological insecurity or because he doesn't want to foist his negativism on the organization, there is pressure on the lower levels to hide their cynicism even if they suspect that the boss is doing so as well. In this case, peer pressures will dictate how much real effort the hidden cynic devotes to personal computing.

The Techno-Type

Some refer to the techno-type as the new breed of management, graduates of business schools where use of Personal Computers is embedded in everyday class work. The technology becomes a natural adjunct to them and they think of a PC not as a box with memory, processing chips, and software, but as an extension of the financial or market analysis part of their job. They turn to the computer as a natural extension of their analytical capability, just as people today use the telephone as a natural extension of their communicating ability.

The cynics are quick to note the benefits of the PC up to a certain level of management, but, at the senior level of management, the job mix changes, emphasizing the intuitive or right-brain functions rather than the analytic or left-brain functions. A manager with a predisposition to the analytic may reach the wrong conclusion by producing an elegant looking business plan which lacks an entrepreneurial perspective.

On the other hand, the techno-types are not limited to recent business school graduates, as pointed out by John Rockart in his article "The CEO Goes On-Line." The article describes the system used by Northwest Industries and its President Ben Heineman (then over 65 years old).

"Northwest's Executive Information System with its extensive and continually growing data base is now used by almost all managers and executives at corporate headquarters to perform their monitoring and analytic functions. But the driving force behind the system and its most significant user remains Heineman. Working with the system is an everyday thing for him, a natural part of his job. With his special knowledge of the business and with his newly acquired ability to write his own programs, Heineman sees great value in working at a terminal himself rather than handing all assignments to staff personnel.

'There is a huge advantage to the CEO to get his hands dirty in the data,' he says, 'because the answers to many significant questions are found in the detail. The system provides me with an improved ability to ask the right questions and to know the wrong answers.' What is more, he finds a comparable advantage in having instant access to the data base to try out an idea he might have. In fact, he has a computer terminal at home and takes another with him on vacations."

The Struggler

Most of the managers I meet and talk to are neither cynics nor techno-types; they are strugglers. They are not graduates of schools where computers were an integral part of the curriculum, but they are readers and observers and are struggling to determine the best level of employment of personal computing for them and for their company. Here are some brief case studies.

- One struggler, an experienced senior financial vice president of a multi-billion dollar pharmaceutical company, states, "Our existing financial systems were developed primarily to comply with good financial and accounting record-keeping and government taxation requirements. This evolution has brought us to the point where many reports are irrelevant to the real information needs of management. Data reported should not be that which is 'easy to collect' or which 'falls out' of operating systems. So why should I get a PC for my office? The data I need isn't in the data base or, if it is, it's not organized the way I need it. My IS people talk to me about playing 'what if' games with my PC. Before I do that, they'll have to tell me 'what is' or even 'what was.'"

■ A marketing vice president of an electrical distributor put it this way: "My people in IS tell me I should get more involved in the process. I have a real conflict, though, and it revolves around time. I go to conferences now and then and I read about IS becoming more strategic and how every executive should have a PC—and soon. Maybe it's true but I've got the same problem as my IS people and it's called *backlog*. Everyone and everything are vying for my time. I've got to learn about the technology in our products and the technology employed by our customers and now I have to learn spreadsheets and decision-support technology. I'd like to help IS and maybe participate on a Steering Committee and take a Lotus course, but I just don't know how to fit it all in and still meet my sales goals this year."

The above is typical of the thoughts of the struggler. He focuses on the gap between what he reads and what he sees in his own company. Furthermore, he worries whether "old dogs" can learn or be taught "new tricks;" and even if it's feasible, how much time does he personally have to spend? He has a full plate now and has less than an hour a day to reflect on new activity; the task of analyzing and learning the techniques to properly employ personal computing looms as a huge mountain waiting to be climbed. That is the struggler's predicament.

End-User Manager's Manifesto

I believe there is really little that can be done for a cynic (whether open or hidden) or a techno-type. It is possible that a cynic can be "converted," but with his experience and predilection, it is unlikely that he would be an enthusiastic user of his own PC, and there is justification for a view that matches his management style and his own capabilities. However, this should not blur his vision on productive personal computing by other managers in the organization or managers who report to him. A bit more familiarity with PCs may improve this vision. It might be healthier if the hidden cynic became an open cynic since the most harmful person to a program is the disbeliever who gives a process lip-service.

As for the techno-type, he must guard against being carried away by the use of technology for its own sake, without sound benefit or economic justification. The newest and the shiniest may not always be the best. However, once the benefits and worth of a project are identified on both management and technical grounds, the techno-type can serve as a good role-model for the company, providing the leading edge and an example for the strugglers to follow.

However, for the struggler, I propose a simple six-step manifesto for improving personal computing perspective and for attaining the proper involvement level. The premise underlying the manifesto is that the management end users of functional departments will have increasing responsibility for information support. Either they will have their own information support group or will be supported by an outside department that looks to them for identification of information needs and establishment of application priorities. In either case, the line manager and his or her people will increasingly use PCs and Executive Workstations. Making a struggler more comfortable with the technology can prove a very positive step; the manifesto to which I now turn is a "starter kit" for this process.

1. *Blend Hard Processes (boxes) with Soft Processes (bubbles)*
A Harvard Business Review article by David Hurst[2] defines two styles of management: one a hard, analytical style symbolized by a box in which actions are based on structure and logical process, and the other a soft, intuitive style symbolized by a bubble in which actions are based more on perspective and feel. The experience of living through a business merger of companies with diametrically opposed management styles convinced Hurst that both types of thinking are needed; the key is to know in which circumstance to employ which style.

It has been my experience that most managers rely on the bubble style of management, their real information emanating more from "walking and talking around" in their personal network, rather than from accessing and analyzing hard data via a Personal Computer. I have read that the average Congressman spends only 14 minutes a day alone, and I believe it is about the same for the average business manager. But the good news is Hurst's conclusion that it is easier to teach a soft-bubble manager the hard-box process than it is to teach the hard-box manager the soft processes. As information technology matures and the concepts of artificial intelligence and expert systems are blended into decision-support systems for management use, a higher premium will be placed on mastering the box style of thinking and managing.

2. *Stay in Front of the Information Curve*

A manager can either manage the technology or be managed by it. In order to avoid the latter, the manager should have a practical handle on his own and his department's information needs. These needs should remain foremost in his mind when dealing with technology and information systems. A popular management concept, that of Critical Success Factors (CSFs), states that there are only a half dozen or so significant areas that, if properly managed, will ensure success. The key is to identify your CSFs and to dedicate your major energy to them and not to the extraneous interrupts that continually occur. Information systems should help measure, support, and shape your CSFs.

CSFs should be used as a benchmark to test suggested changes to existing systems or proposals for new ones. The question should be what impact does the proposals have on CSFs? If the manager fails to ask this, he is at the mercy of the "technocrats" who can provide so many kinds of hardware and software products that a condition can develop called "option shock." As someone said, we are quickly faced with "insurmountable opportunities."

3. *Put Your Toe in the Technological Water*

While even the cynic should try out the technology, if only to further support his belief, for the struggler it is essential. The most practical first step is to try a spreadsheet package, probably Lotus 1-2-3 since it is the most widely used. You'll have to decide whether your instructional style is better served by reading a manual, following an interactive diskette, or signing up for a one-day, hands-on tutorial. It's not going to be easy, but just that realization is worth the price and time of the instruction. The novice should not be surprised to find that it will take as much as 40 hours of work to feel comfortable with Lotus.

There is real benefit, however, from manipulating spreadsheets personally. There are unexpected results to some problems. For example, a 30 percent forecasting error may only mean a 5 percent increase in inventory, when intuitively it would appear greater. Other pertinent relationships can often be uncovered when working spreadsheets in an interactive mode. Also, graphical relationships may provide a new perspective to data representation. With tomorrow's manager taking responsibility for much of his or her information support and with software becoming slowly, but progressively, easier for managers to use, it is vital to have hands-on experience with the basic information tools.

4. *Focus on the Front End of the Process – The "What" and "Why"*
This may appear to contradict the previous recommendation, but the manager, for the most part, should avoid the "how" of information systems and concentrate on the "what" and "why." The pertinent questions are "What do I want done?" (the specification) and "Why do I want it done?" (the benefit or return on investment). When one is deep in an information systems discussion or meeting, it is a useful check to ask, "Are we working on the what and why questions?" If not, at best you are probably wasting your time by delving into areas where you cannot contribute, or at worst making a potentially counter-productive contribution.

While there are benefits from learning how to produce your own spreadsheets, it is not necessary to program your own formulas. A possible compromise is to learn to build your own spreadsheets for purposes of computer literacy, but then delegate subsequent ones to individuals who use the technology on a more regular basis. Otherwise, you could find yourself spending an inordinate amount of time on what is really irrelevant to you, on the "how" versus the "what" and "why" questions. As someone aptly put it, when we focus on the technology, on the "how," we become like "the stereo enthusiast who, tantalized by tracking errors, wild over woofers, intrigued by intermodulation, and delirious over decibels, doesn't enjoy music."

5. *Use Personal Computing Prototype Mode*
Stating that the manager should develop his own information system specification is often not enough. The manager may not have the vision at the outset to define exactly what it is he or she needs. One hears the lament "don't give me what I said, give me what I meant." While eventually the production version of the application may be developed by the IS staff, a simplified prototype version can be supplied to the manager for his manipulation and use. The

application may involve accessing data from the corporate data base using a management-oriented fourth-generation language. The beauty of the prototype is that the manager can try out different options before the significant investment is made in developing the final version. It is an accepted fact that the earlier an error is caught, the less the expense to correct it.

The prototyping concept, along with low-cost personal computing, permits the element of experimentation in information systems. One would assume that this has always been a natural characteristic of information systems but such has not been the case. Heretofore, there was considerable risk in a major development project: the application might not meet specifications, it might be too difficult to use, or it might not be useful at all. Now an impractical application can be abandoned before the investment makes it impossible or impolitic to do so. And more important, things can be tried that can materially improve the competitive position of a company—and with manageable risk.

6. *Maintain a High Degree of Patience*

Finally, though systems are being made more user-friendly, the industry has a way to go, and a manager should, therefore, exhibit a high degree of patience. I liken the situation to that of my dog Sammie who formerly bit the hands of my friends who came into our house. After severe admonishment and training, Sammie now only nips their hands; someone, like myself, who has seen the progress, would call this behavior "user-friendly."

We are already in the second generation, some say the third, of spreadsheet software. Multiplan is a great deal easier to use than VisiCalc while some claim Lotus and Jazz are still-easier to use. Yet, *I* would say that these packages are user-friendly only if the user is an accountant or other type of professional; when the user is a manager it's a different story.

While the cause of some of the difficulty can be placed at the door of the IS department because it didn't select the right software or deliver the proper training, indoctrination, and individual consulting, the end-user manager hasn't been blameless. Managers often have acquired PCs and PC software directly from computer stores or via a salesman without checking with IS. This "go-it-alone" attitude has resulted in a good bit of wheel-reinvention. In light of all this, it is suggested that the manager try patiently to "pat Sammie" a few times more.

Conclusion

This then is an end-user manager's manifesto. It is based on personal observation and the analysis of research projects on the management use of Personal Computers. I have delineated four types of management users: the open cynic, the hidden cynic, the techno-type, and the struggler. Much has been written and said about the use of Personal Computers by professionals, administrators, and clerical personnel, but not as much about their use by managers. The result is that many managers are using PCs in the same way as the people who work for them. Typing one's own letters or becoming a spreadsheet whiz are not the real pay-off areas. If, instead, managers use PCs to support their unique managerial activities, they will, I am convinced, benefit the most.

References

1. Rockart, John. "The CEO Goes Online." *Harvard Business Review,* Jan-Feb. 1982.
2. Hurst, David K. "Of Boxes, Bubbles and Effective Management." *Harvard Business Review,* May-June 1984.

6. IS Long-Range Planning

"The trouble with planning is that it has a tendency to deteriorate into work."

Planning a job or a project before launching it is a logical and practical way to effectively carry out an assignment. While individuals and companies realize the worth of planning specific tasks and projects, the application of planning to a major and complex function of a business is not as readily seen. Projects usually have a one- or two-year time frame, while planning for a major department or function like IS requires a longer time frame, usually in the three- to five-year range. It is surprising, therefore, that with the need for a long-term focus, examples of effective, comprehensive five-year IS plans are not more prevalent.

Evolutionary Phases

Within most companies, planning has gone through an evolution consistent with the concept of information systems growth. It is not just an IS issue, but a corporate one as well. Managers have always been leery of planning. Planning is hard work, not much fun, ill-defined, not immediately rewarding, and can detract from time devoted to the day-to-day operations of the business. Also, the classic type A executive has a natural aversion to the planning function. He is an action-oriented, aggressive leader with short attention span, who is impatient with activities that don't appear to have concrete, immediate payoffs. Planning is just not in the natural mind-set of the type A manager. As a result, the period of the late 50's and early 60's provided a corporate environment that was unreceptive to planning. Since any IS planning methodology must match and fit the company culture, it was obviously not a good time to do much serious thinking about developing an IS long-range plan.

The late 60's and most of the 70's might be characterized as a complacency era with corporate leaders exhibiting a laissez-faire attitude towards planning. Executives realized that planning was necessary but they really didn't know how or what to do. It certainly didn't require much of their personal attention, they conjectured. During this period, managers gave lip service to planning, perfunctorily nodding whenever the subject came up.

53

A sharp dichotomy between planning and doing was drawn, with planners assigned full-time to the task but separated in an ivory tower environment where they would work and not interfere with the non-planners (the workers). During this time, impressive documents were produced and put on the shelf where they gathered dust, except when withdrawn to display to visiting consultants, auditors, college professors, or planners from other companies. These thick tomes were quite impressive but did not really direct strategies and actions.

The 80's brought a new concept — action planning, planning that is jointly conducted by executives and planners, that addresses the key business directions of the company, and is followed and modified as market changes dictate. The plan is the basis for action, not simply a book put on the shelf for review by the intelligentsia.

What caused this new and serious look at planning is a bit obscure. It may have been the inflationary economy and its impact on future growth; it may have been the political changes in regulation, taxes and budgetary direction; it may have been the emergence of foreign competition and particularly the Japanese model of doing business based on a long-term planning foundation. Or it just could have been an awakening on the part of executives to the importance of looking out further and the realization that they had to be involved in the process. Whatever the cause or causes, it has become evident that a manager's job and the success of his or her enterprise are dependent on a duality of responsibility — the responsibility to perform to the current year's goals and the responsibility to plan to meet future years' goals. This establishes a healthy and receptive corporate environment for IS planning.

In the early stages of IS, applications were initiated and implemented as separate entities without much attention to integration. The pressure was to get a specific application up and running to satisfy a particular user's need. The first manifestation of planning was *project planning,* for it was found that many of the earlier applications did not really satisfy the user needs once the implementation was completed. Users would say, "that isn't what I told you" or "you should have done what I meant, not what I said." Projects typically were completed behind schedule and took more resources than were contemplated — and often by a great margin. It soon became clear that identifying the project milestones, gaining user sign-off on specifications, and scheduling management reviews throughout the cycle produced better products.

The proliferation of applications during the "contagion stage" resulted in heavy demands for computer time. This initiated the second kind of IS planning, *capacity planning*. Though, to this day, capacity planning remains more art than science, IS managers had to find a way to project future computer hardware requirements in an era of growing application backlogs. Through capacity planning, the current workload could be modeled in order to project volume levels and hardware needs.

With the increase in computer resources, management became alarmed over the sharply rising cost of data processing services. This led to a third type of planning, *resource* or *budgetary planning*. IS managers began developing annual operational plans which necessitated looking ahead at least a year to project what hardware, software, people, and facilities were required to run the operation and handle the growing portfolio of computer applications. This ushered in the "control stage" of IS development.

The advent of the "integration stage" of IS brought the realization that applications have been developed in a fragmentary way. An assessment of management needs showed a requirement for integrated data files to provide meaningful management information to run the business. This established the need for another type of planning, *long-range planning,* to map the direction and strategy of the IS function to support the business in the next three- to five-year period.

Principles of Planning

In order to discuss the content of an IS long-range plan, we'll first have to look at some underlying principles.

- *Planning is a verb not a noun.* The implication here is that planning is not a once-a-year function that produces a report and gets management blessing. Rather it is a continuous process that takes place throughout the year. The report is reviewed and updated continually; it is a "living" document. Most planners and executives would agree that the effectiveness of planning is in the process rather than in the final document.

- *The IS plan must be consistent with the corporate business plan.* Since the IS plan supports the future business, the future business direction of the company must be known before any meaningful IS plan can be developed. This usually means that the planning cycle for IS is in sequence with the corporate planning cycle. A set of corporate strategic guidelines should provide the basis for the planning cycle for the year. The IS cycle should commence at that point and coincide with the key management review points of the corporate schedule.

- *Management involvement and commitment are essential.* In order to achieve this involvement, management should be included in the review process as part of an information steering committee. Since each manager is involved in his own department plan, conservative and sensitive use of his time is important. Meetings should be well-structured and focused on broad strategic issues rather than short-term tactical ones. The make-up and operation of the management review board or steering committee is extremely important to an effective plan. Obviously, the content of the plan is critical, but its perception by management can also be crucial.

- *Planning is everybody's job.* Though a specific individual may be responsible for developing the IS plan, he or she is merely the "agent," chartered to select a planning methodology and to ensure that the planning process takes place according to that methodology and consistent with corporate guidelines. Though the individual can contribute to the content of the plan, he alone is not responsible for it. The key department managers and the IS executive must provide the strategic directional content of the plan. Planning is not a function to be delegated. Organizational behaviorists point out that it is difficult for a manager to successfully implement a plan that was dictated from above. The concept of grassroots planning, where the people responsible for implementing the plan are also involved in the planning process, has proved a more workable concept. Achieving "ownership" is the critical element.

- *It takes several cycles to institutionalize a planning process.* As already stated, planning is not an easy task and runs against the grain of the action-oriented, hard-driving manager. Therefore, no matter how sound the methodology chosen or how efficient the techniques for developing the plan, it will take more than one iteration to establish the process firmly within a company. Planners instituting the process should not be discouraged the first time around. Often the first year's plan is one that is not completely understood and "bought" by either the IS people implementing it or the IS users supported by the plan. An assessment should be made at the completion of the first planning cycle in order to improve the process during the next cycle. Modifications may include items such as an offsite, half-day workshop to review the final version, changing the composition of the steering committee, or transposing various milestones. Remember, the first premise is that planning should be seen as a verb not a noun. It is a continuous process.

The Long-Range Plan

Figure 1 divides the contents of an IS long-range plan into 15 categories.

Figure 1
Contents of
an IS Plan

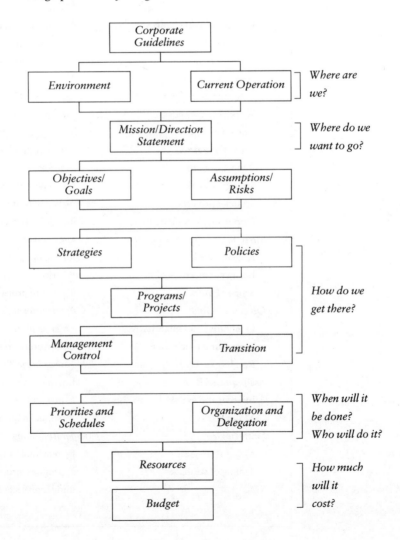

The plan answers the six basic questions that should be addressed by any long-range plan: Where are we? Where do we want to go? How do we get there? When will it be done? Who will do it? How much will it cost? While the contents of the IS plan will differ based on particular companies, particular IS groups, and the stage of development, Figure 2 presents a good starting point for our discussion.

Figure 2
IS Plan Contents

Corporate Guidelines
  Strategic—markets/products
  Volume indicators
  Organizational changes
Environment
  Industry trends
  Technology scan
  Government regulations
  Workforce composition
  Customer/supplier relations
Current Operations
  Budget/organization
  Strengths/weaknesses
  Strategy/projects
  Opportunities/potentials
Mission/Direction Statement
  Reason for IS
  Business/objectives of IS
  Scope of users
Objectives/Goals
  Qualitative and quantitative
  Targets and time frame
  Results expected
Assumptions/Risks
  Internal and external constraints
  Major risks
Strategies
  Major strategies
  Timing of strategies

Policies
  Major current policies (internal
    and external to IS)
  Projected changes and time frame
Programs/Projects
  Current programs/projects
  New programs required
Management Control Techniques
  New procedures/methods needed
  Timing and approach to develop
    new techniques
Transition Plans
  Old environment
  New environment
  Transitional procedures
  User and operational conditioning
Priorities and Schedules
  Prioritization of projects
  Timing of projects
Organization and Delegation
  Organization to manage IS
  Delegation of responsibility
Resource Projections
  Equipment/software/facilities
    projections
  Personnel requirements
Operating Budget
  Incremental budget by new
    program/project or zero-based
  Budget projected for each year

Some sections will be emphasized one year and de-emphasized another. For example, at a particular development stage, the establishment of IS management control techniques may be of principal significance, while downplayed in subsequent years. This is also true for areas such as policies or transition plans.

Often planners feel that if a plan doesn't change dramatically each year, it is not a good one or they are not doing their job. This is not the case, because if a good solid look at the future is taken with meaningful, well-founded strategies then put in place, plans may hold with but minor fine-tuning for the next several years. An extremely useful technique is to develop a "difference document" which summarizes the key changes of this year's plan from the next year's. Management should be particularly interested in this perspective.

■

Conclusion

There are many jokes concerning planning; it is fair game to those, and there are many, who exhibit a degree of skepticism toward the art. Someone said that planning at his company means, "when you lose sight of your objectives, redouble your efforts." Another manager I know describes his company's planning style as characterized by the phrase "ready, fire, aim." Jokes aside, the time has come to take a serious look at IS planning. If indeed IS has switched from a role of "supporting the business" to "being the business" with distributed, online systems as the catalyst, it behooves the IS executive to recognize this and to plan for it. An IS department without a long-range plan will become a business anachronism; with such a plan, the course has been chartered.

7. Using Critical Success Factors to Set Information System Priorities

"There is nothing quite so useless as doing with great efficiency that which should not be done at all." – *Peter Drucker*

The key result of an information systems plan is a prioritization of the applications to be implemented—in fact, this may be the definition of information systems planning. For what is more important than determining what resources should be expended on which projects and in what priority. The approach used here is to marry the critical success factor concept with a four-criteria application prioritization scheme.

Critical Success Factors

Critical Success Factors (CSFs) are the few key areas of activity in which favorable results are absolutely necessary for a company to reach its goals. The concept was developed by Dr. John Rockart of MIT[1] for both internal information resource plans and to assist major enterprises in assessing their managerial information needs. Because these areas of activity are critical, the manager should have the appropriate information to allow him to determine whether events are proceeding sufficiently well in each area. The CSF method provides a structured technique to extract information of high demand by virtue of its identification with critical business activities.

Figure 1 schematically describes the CSF process. Only by identifying the critical success factors will the managers know what information is indispensable to their leadership role.

Objectives or goals are the "ends," usually stated in the form of numbers such as Revenue Dollars, Sales Volume, etc. CSFs are the means to the ends. For example, a golfer may want to shoot a 78 on a particular day. That's a goal. Since the golfer's problem is driving, the critical success factor in this case would be hitting fairways off the tee. Concentrating on that area is critical in reaching his goal of a 78.

Another example is a supermarket chain. In addition to store location, the business has four success factors: product mix, inventory, price, and promotion. When these four activities are managed well in all stores, then the supermarket chain prospers. Their impact is therefore "critical." The measures or information attributes concerning product mix, inventory, price, and promotion become critical in their own right. Efforts to organize these measures for automated processing lead to high-priority IS projects.

Figure 1
The Critical
Success Factor
Process

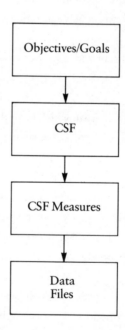

The Three-Stage Process

Figure 2 illustrates the recommended three-stage CSF approach which can lead to the establishment of application priorities. The process involves:

1. A management briefing of 2 to 3 hours where the CSF concept is described and illustrated

2. The interview of two levels of management to determine their conceptions of the CSFs (described below)

3. A "focusing" workshop (also described below)

As shown in Figure 2, there are four possible results of the process. We examine *here* only the fourth—establishing application priorities.

Figure 2
Using Critical
Success Factors

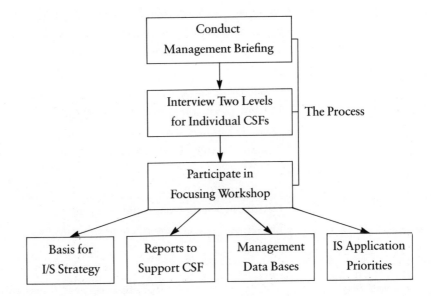

63

The Interview Process

A structured questionnaire technique is used to gather the necessary information from 20 to 30 key managers, including top management. It is suggested that a letter explaining the CSF process be sent to the selected managers in advance of the interview. The interview should last approximately 1 to 1½ hours. The results of the interview should be typed and returned to the interviewee for his or her review and edit. Figure 3 shows a sample interview form.

Figure 3
Sample Interview Form

Interviewee:_____ Title:_____

Division:_____ Years with Company:_____ Time in Present Position:_____

Interviewer:_____ Recorder:_____ Date:_____

A. *Job function/responsibilities*
  - Describe principal job responsibilities, place in organization
  - State job goals

B. *Critical success factors (CSFs)*
  - Identify areas crucial to the success of the business
  - Identify information necessary to support CSFs

C. *Problem identification priority*
  - List and prioritize information problems
  - Quantify benefits for each problem resolution
  - Describe difficulty (time, cost, technology) in resolving problem

D. *Future information needs*
  - Describe how technology could alter your job
  - List future (2-5 years) information requirements

The Focusing Workshop

The objectives of a "focusing workshop" are well-described by John Rockart and Adam Crescenzi in an issue of the Sloan Management Review? They conducted a CSF study with the top management of Southwestern Ohio Steel (SOS) of Hamilton, Ohio, one of the top three steel service centers in the United States. Tom Heldman is SOS's Chief Financial

Officer and Jacque Huber is its Vice President of Sales. Rockart and Crescenzi describe the focusing workshop as follows:

"Preparation for the focusing workshop on management's part consists of reading interview summaries, which are then distributed after they have been reviewed by the individual participants. At the workshop, the consultants present a 'strawman' of corporate mission, objectives, and CSFs—all constructed from the analysis of the introductory workshop and interviews. The strawman provides a basis for extended, often intense, discussion and the key to uncover varying perceptions and disagreements among the management team. This is the most significant and difficult step in the first phase, for different individual perspectives, managerial loyalties, and desires emerge. Thus, leadership by corporate management is essential in untangling the myriad of differences and focusing on the core elements of the business. The end result is agreement on what the company's missions and goals are.

During the focusing workshop, corporate objectives developed in the introductory workshop were reaffirmed. Most of these objectives were related to financial and marketing aspects of the business. From a set of forty initially suggested CSFs obtained through the interviews, four emerged:

- *Maintaining excellent supplier relationships*

- *Maintaining or improving customer relationships*

- *Merchandising available inventory to its most value-added use*

- *Utilizing available capital and human resources efficiently and effectively*

As Tom Heldman notes: 'This is the key meeting. The interviews are merely a preliminary: a softening-up process in which managers get an initial opportunity to think deeply about the corporation, as well as to develop relationships with the consultants.'

In the course of the focusing workshop, what had previously been implicit was made explicit—sometimes with surprising, insightful results. In Jacque Huber's words: 'We all knew what was critical for our company, but the discussion—sharing and agreeing—was really important. What came out of it was a minor revelation. Seeing it on the blackboard in black and white is much more significant than carrying around a set of ideas which are merely intuitively felt.'

Although the interpersonal skills and business knowledge of the consulting team running the focusing workshop are very significant, the workshop technique itself readily captures the attention and involvement of the management team and eases the seminar leadership job. Again, Heldman sums it up: 'Focusing on what makes the company a success intrigued almost all of top management. It appealed to a group of good managers, allowing them to engage in a discussion of what they knew best and what seemed important to them.'"

■

Application Priority Analysis

Once the interviews are completed, the various critical information application areas are identified and prioritized in accordance with a four-criteria evaluation basepoint: 1) return on investment, 2) risk, 3) impact, and 4) demand. The first two criteria are given weights of 20 while the latter two have weights of 10, for maximum score of 60. Weights can be adjusted, however, in accordance with a company's perspective on the issues. This is the way it works.

Return on Investment

This criterion is probably the most tangible and measurable of the four. The accepted criterion for measuring ROI is discounted cash flow which, in essence, follows the principle that near-term dollars are worth more than longer-term dollars because of the interest value of money. This table is based on the company's accepted rate of return.

ROI	Weight
2 times acceptable rate	20
1½ times acceptable rate	15
Acceptable rate	10
½ times acceptable rate	5

If the company's acceptable rate of return is 30% before tax, then an ROI of 30% scores 10 points, while a rate of 45% scores 15, and a rate of 60% or above scores 20. On the downside an ROI of 15% scores 5 points.

Risk

This criterion is based on the relative risk of the application working and being implemented on time and within budget. Three elements of risk are evaluated: size, flexibility, and technology. With this criterion, if the risk is high, the weight is low and vice versa. *Size* is a measurement of the man-years and development-dollars. *Flexibility* is a measure of the structure and familiarity of the application in question – the higher the flexibility (i.e., the less structure), the greater the risk. *Technology* reflects the extent that a particular application requires new hardware and software or untested techniques. The following table assigns the points based on three elements.

Risk Elements	Weight
All three factors high	0
Two factors high	5
One factor high	10
All factors low	20

Impact

This criterion measures the degree of benefit emanating from successful completion of the application. Although these benefits may be intangible, their impact is often significant for the long or short term. Such benefits can bring a company a competitive advantage (see Essay 2) in improved customer service or enhanced employee morale – areas difficult to quantify. The following matrix indicates a method for assigning the 10-point weight of this element.

Benefits/Significance	Weight
Long-Term Benefits, Moderate Significance	1
Short-Term Benefits, Moderate Significance	4
Long-Term Benefits, High Significance	7
Short-Term Benefits, High Significance	10

Demand

This criterion reflects the demand for the application within the organization. It is a measure of who wants it and the extent of the demand. The following matrix indicates how to assign the 10-point weight to the application.

Demanded by	Weight
3 or more top managers	10
The president or key executive	7
6 or more key middle managers	4
A single sponsor	1

Sample Use of Priority Analysis

The table below illustrates the use of application priority for a particular company. It is obvious that it takes a good deal of subjective judgment to place weights on the various factors but, nonetheless, the method offers a systematic and consistent approach for determining the order in which applications should be computerized.

Application	Factors				Totals
	ROI	Risk	Impact	Demand	
Integrated Financials	18	10	7	8	43
Product Line Reporting	14	13	8	5	40
Sales Forecasting	12	14	7	6	39
Sales/Customer Analysis	9	18	5	4	36
LOB Production Scheduling	13	6	6	6	31
Financial Modeling	8	8	6	4	26
Spreadsheet Budgets	5	9	3	4	21
Truck Loading/Routing	4	11	3	2	20

Using the CSF Approach

The process as described below can be completed in 6 weeks. A major part of the time is spent in interviewing, compiling the interviews, and reviewing the results with those being interviewed. This part of the process can be condensed, but it has been found that schedules of busy managers usually do not permit an uninterrupted orderly sequence.

Week(s)	Activity
1	Select and train team; hold management workshop
2-3	Conduct interviews with key managers
4	Participate in focusing workshop with key managers
5	Review and analyze interviews and workshop results; develop priority analysis
6	Write report and present to management

Many benefits accrue from this straightforward approach, the most significant of which is obtaining a top-down judgment of the direction for information applications. Everyone cannot have his or her application as "number 1," but at least all will know the process and have participated in it. There is a greater sense of ownership of the results through this method than through others which are more IS- or technology-driven.

References

1. Rockart, John F. "Chief Executives Define Own Information Needs," *Harvard Business Review*, March-April 1979.
2. Rockart, John F., and Crescenzi, Adam D. "Engaging Top Management in Information Technology." *MIT Sloan Management Review*, Summer 1984.

8. Developing an Information Systems Architecture

■

"When your only tool is a hammer, the whole world begins to look like a nail."

The thirty years of commercial data processing have been turbulent and most industry pundits forecast that this climate will continue. Companies have gone through cycles in their use of data processing—from small, individually run computer centers to large, highly centralized complexes and more recently to decentralized or distributed data processing. Many feel that we are in the era of the end user with the management of information being turned over to functional users; others see a mild step back toward more centralization as the needs for integration, intra-company, and inter-company data exchange become more evident—and all this is happening in an environment of a technology blitz with more products than ever before.

Increasingly, managers, including the CEO, are beginning to worry about their company's IS resource and its ability to respond to a combination of increasing technological options, changing business conditions brought about by deregulation, new products and services, increased competition, and changing economic, political and social conditions. Both IS people and user/managers are beginning to look for the "port in the storm," the "hook to hang your hat on," or whatever analogy you choose to describe the situation. Having an information systems architecture can provide such a "hook."

■

Information Systems Architecture as a Unifying Force

Cornelius H. Sullivan, Jr.[1] defined architecture as "an effort to achieve fit or harmony between form and context." The architect designs a street, a building, a city (the form) that meets the requirements of the people (the context). The context includes the financial resources, building and health codes, and environmental constraints. The success of the architecture is measured by the fit of form and context. There is, of course, a time dimension

71

involved: the architect must take a look at population trends and traffic growth so that his architecture adapts to a future context as well as a current one.

The analogy holds for the information systems architect. The form differs as does the context, but the objective remains the same—to find a meaningful fit between the two. The information systems architect, like the building architect, faces the challenge of the past. Information systems, like buildings and streets, just grew. Pressures of time and cost favored alterations, add-ons, extensions, patches, and the like. The conflict arises when the context becomes so demanding and volatile that the form finally does not possess the flexibility to respond at all.

This is what is referred to as "biting-the-bullet time." Let's consider an example. Several years ago traffic on Boston's Southeast Expressway had increased to a point where refurbishment was mandatory (patches would no longer do and more lanes were needed). The form no longer fit the context. Boston commuters had to spend more time or take another route while a new architecture was being developed. As in a building, we don't like to break down an "outside" wall. But if we run out of temporary inside walls to modify, there's no other choice. A well-thought-out IS architecture minimizes the demolition of outside walls.

Developing an information systems architecture that matches form and context is becoming top-priority for IS executives and is gaining the attention of senior management as well. An architecture which can handle the complexities of today's business yet provide the built-in flexibility and expandability to incorporate tomorrow's growth and new requirements is necessary; its development is no mean task.

Architecture Context

A good starting point for building a framework that defines the architectural context is the classic Anthony Triangle[2] (Figure 1).

Figure 1
The Anthony Triangle

The company's operational control activities consist of day-to-day business transactions like order processing, purchasing, and accounts payable. The management control activities are those that assist the management of operational activities and include functions like production scheduling, financial reporting, and inventory control. The strategic planning activities look at the external world and the development of market and product strategies that can achieve a prescribed set of sales, revenue, profit, and return on investment (ROI).

A key need of information systems architecture is for integration. If every individual or every department worked independently, architectural planning would be greatly simplified—but this is not the case. Personal computer users within a company may start with freestanding applications only to discover that they require data from another department, the corporate data base, or a data source outside the company.

Four "dimensions" or levels of integration must be considered in developing an information systems architecture: vertical, horizontal, geographic Intra-Company, and geographic Inter-Company.

1. *Vertical Integration*

   Vertical integration, as illustrated in Figure 2, is based on the typical organization of a company into functional activities or processes such as engineering, manufacturing, or marketing.

Figure 2
Vertical Integration

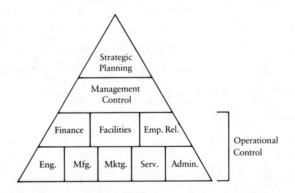

Vertical integration implies that activity is managed and controlled by successive layers of management responsible for that function. For example, salesmen report to sales managers, who report to sales directors, who report to a sales or marketing vice president. Much of the data supports a specific function and is significant only to that function. If this were exclusively so throughout the organization, the information system architectural context would be built around separate data base supporting each functional area. We know, of course, that this is not the case.

2. *Horizontal Integration*

It is a given, except in very rare cases, that no function exists as an island within an organization; there is strong horizontal connection between functions. For example, the engineering design of a product results in a bill of materials which Manufacturing uses to build the product. Marketing forecasts and orders are prerequisites for establishing the production schedule and inventory levels that Manufacturing requires to fill customer orders.

Finance, Facility Management, and Employee Relations are support and service organizations which illustrate another type of horizontal integration. Although a specific personnel complement might be assigned to service each functional area, the personnel policies, procedures, and employee benefit programs are usually centralized and generally standard across the total organization.

Most companies have multiple products or services which cut across the functional boundaries. These cross-functional products are called product lines or business units. They are headed by a product line manager or business unit manager who has profit responsibility for the unit. This type of horizontal integration is normally referred to as a "matrix-type management" structure (Figure 3). The functional units, in effect, have two bosses: the functional manager and the product/business manager. Analogously, information systems architecture must support this two-way split (i.e., accommodate both the vertical and horizontal needs for information).

Figure 3
Horizontal Integration

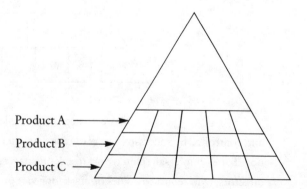

Product A
Product B
Product C

3. *Geographic (Intra-Company) Integration*

    Geography is a vital integration element and obviously must be carefully considered as a contextual factor in the architecture. The intra-company dimension pertains to relationships within the enterprise as opposed to relationships with outside enterprises. Companies have remote sales offices, corporate facilities, manufacturing operations, and service units. Their roles and responsibilities must be analyzed as to their fit in the organization and whether they are part of the functional activity, the business unit activity, or both. Geography may mean across the parking lot, across the city, across the country, or across the world. Geographic integration obviously is a very volatile factor, usually changing more often than either vertical or horizontal integration.

4. *Geographic (Inter-Company) Integration*

    Inter-company integration is the linkage with institutions or agencies that are not under the direct control of the company. A trend in information systems is to use information systems technology to develop inter-corporate connections. For example, an electrical distributor might have terminals in the purchasing offices of its key customers. The terminals communicate directly to the host company's data base, producing inventory status, ship dates, prices, and the like. In addition, the distributor may have terminals that link to its major vendor's data base, providing similar information.

    Architecture must also take into account requirements imposed by outside agencies whether they be the Internal Revenue Service, Office of Safety and Health, or the variety of regulatory agencies. Usually these requirements would be met with by-products of existing data bases or applications, rather than separate system entities.

    Another example of inter-company integration is online access to the more than 2500 current external data bases (up from 400 just 5 years ago).[3] The type of data ranges from financial information and investment statistics to market and planning data. The objective is to integrate the data from outside sources with pertinent internal data to develop strategic investment or marketing strategies.

Certainly, the integration issue is an overriding one in establishing an effective information systems architecture. Often only close scrutiny can reveal just what data bases and data flows are required for a desired level of integration. But the political and cultural factors within a company are as important as the technical factors—probably more so. People are the ultimate contextual element.

The people constituting the organization motivate it. They provide the political and cultural energies that we might identify as "driving" forces.

One driving force may be an *efficiency motivation*—information systems budgets have grown so big and so fast that the prime motivation is to contain the costs. A company may feel that it is spending too much for what it is receiving.

Or the driving force may be a *control motivation*—management feels that the technology has taken over, micros and workstations are showing up all over the place, everyone has his or her own data files, and no system communicates with any other. It's an environment of "technological clutter."

On the other hand, the company climate may foster an *effectiveness motivation*—a realization that information systems technology can play an increasingly significant role in the business and indeed can be the dominant force enabling a company to remain competitive. In this mode, IS is considered a future investment in the same way as an investment in plant, building, and research and development. It's a longer-term view of information as a critical resource.

Lastly, the driving force may be a *decentralization motivation*—based on the view that the information systems function has always been a fortress unto itself with the moats being huge backlogs and inordinately poor response times. Managers are tired of waiting and want to act; they want responsibility for satisfying their own information needs, establishing priorities, assigning resources, and deciding how much they will pay for information services.

Of course, it is vitally important to determine the driving forces within the company. You may not agree with them but you'd best be aware of them before tackling the architecture issue.

Architecture Form

The form of an information systems architecture involves logical elements and physical elements. The logical elements include the rules and procedures and the guiding principles by which the company operates, such as security and privacy, standards and protocol, financial and personnel policies. These logical elements are important boundaries and constraints to information systems architecture.

The four physical architecture building blocks are: Applications, Data/Information, Hardware/Software Processing Platforms, and Communications (the Network).

1. *Applications*

The application building block provides the direct interface to the primary architectural context, namely the people. Because of this, it is the starting point of architectural development. Applications in the broadest sense are everything the system provides to its users. Applications emanate from a comprehensive information needs assessment. A necessary prerequisite is a thorough understanding of the company's contextual framework — what goes on at the three levels of the Anthony Triangle. Applications accommodate all activities of the triangle, from order processing and inventory control at the operational level, to financial reports and tracking documents at the management control level, to business modeling and strategic forecasting at the strategic planning level.

A shared vision of the current and future applications portfolio that supports and shapes the strategic direction of the business is the cornerstone of information systems architecture.

2. *Data/Information*

Though data is often defined as unprocessed numbers and words (similar to raw material in a production operation) and information as processed numbers and words (finished goods), the terms are often used interchangeably. The collection of data is the foundation of applications and its care, tending, and feeding is of paramount significance. Data is the mortar of information systems and is a key architectural element. Data and its interrelations must be determined by a mapping against the business activities or processes.

Figure 4 places a logical or conceptual data base structure next to the activity triangle. It suggests factors to consider in developing the data/information portion of an architecture. Generally, there are a number of subject data bases. As indicated in Figure 4, some form of integrated transaction data base(s) exists, as well as a variety of subject data bases.

Management control and strategic functions require only summary or cumulative information, usually not on a repetitive or real-time basis such that separate data bases are usually provided for their use. External data bases are tapped to provide data outside the direct control of the company but required to develop meaningful company strategies. Again, the degree of integration required and the application portfolio determine the data base make-up.

Figure 4
Subject Data Bases

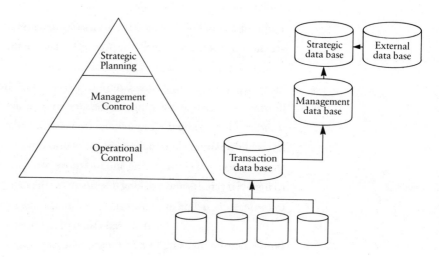

3. *Hardware/Software Processing Platforms*

Not too many years ago, hardware/software processing platforms were the elements that came to mind most frequently when architecture was mentioned. This is not the case anymore, though they do play a significant role. Now, the application and information/data dimension precede the computer system in architectural priorities. But, it is also true that the three are related; both the application packages and data base software influence the selection of computer hardware.

The hardware platform(s) are the engines that support the architecture and provide the processing power. The selection involves careful calibration and forecasting of the processing capability required and its best physical deployment. This is where the centralized/decentralized concept comes into play, determining whether the "processing boxes" should be placed close to the point of transaction (departmental function) or at some intermediate or central point. The decision must be tempered by a host of cost and efficiency trade-offs, such as communication costs vs. processing costs and use of micro vs. mini vs. mainframe.

Similarly, the selection of systems software is an integral part of the processing platform. Included are operating systems, transaction processing software, data base management software (tied very closely to the data dimension), and communication software. Systems software, the layer upon which application systems are built, obviously must be selected with a great deal of understanding of its fit within the overall architecture.

4. *Communications/Network*

Communications provide the delivery service linking the first three elements. Architecture involves the development of a communications network that accepts transaction data and management requests for information, and delivers responses to the many systems users at each remote physical business entity. The decisions here include selection of communications channels, carriers, protocols, capacity, response time, and so on. The options are many, whether one is looking at inter-building communications involving some sort of local area network, or inter-city communications using a wide area network.

Communications considerations normally involve linking computer use at three levels of the organization. The first is the *personal level* where an individual utilizes information processing to satisfy such personal needs as calendars and schedules, word processing, or spreadsheet analysis. The second is the *department level,* where individuals share common peripherals and data bases, to communicate among themselves in performing departmental business. The third is the *enterprise level* where individuals and departments link to corporate information or communicate to carry out a task for the total organization. Communications architecture provides for the current and projected needs at these three levels. Since it also must provide for any inter-company communications, the design of the communications network requires a high level of technical expertise and experience.

Architecture Groundrules

An architectural framework has been presented based on the definition of architecture as a fit between context and form. The elements of context and form have been described, with the warning that both are in a state of rapid change. Information systems design itself is far from a mature discipline. Thus, the challenge is to carve out an architecture in an environment where the essential elements are in flux. Following are some groundrules to consider.

- *Focus on a Future Vision.*   An architecture cannot be built on the linear extrapolation of the past. Instead, a shared vision of the future must serve as a target. The information system architecture must be based on the kind of business operation that is envisioned and the prevailing strategies, future directions, and growth patterns. It should depict where you want to be, not where you are. Only after you know where you want to be, can you develop strategies on "how to get there from here."

- *Consider Architecture as the Top-Priority Job.*   Though most challenging and difficult, developing an architecture is the most important single task for an information systems function. Because it has proven so illusive, IS groups have opted to proceed a piece at a time, without an overall design. While this method satisfies the short-term requirements, a serious price is paid in the long run. Patches can be put in place to keep a system in operation, but they are only temporary expedients. Sooner or later, an "outside wall" must be knocked down.

- *Maintain a High Degree of Flexibility.*   Despite a serious effort to project a shared vision of the future, it is still difficult to be exact because of the conditions cited above. Thus, the architect must provide considerable systems flexibility, to build an open-ended architecture that can accommodate as many options as possible. This is particularly true in areas such as information management and communications, where standards and common protocols have yet to be established.

- *Don't Introduce Constraints Prematurely.*   It is also important that the initial design be logical rather than physical. The architecture, like a city planning design, implies the general specifications for the types of materials to be used but rarely specifies brand names or exact composition. The benefits are twofold. First, the conceptual design is not limited by the constraints inherent in a particular hardware architecture, data base management system, etc. Second, the design is open-ended and provides leeway for the implementers to use the most cost-effective materials and to take advantage of improvements and advancements in the physical technology.

■ *Consider the Audience.* Because of the scope and the need to ensure acceptance of the architecture design in the corporate culture, multiple perspectives must be presented. For the end-user, the perspective should provide an understanding of the system behavior as it relates to the user interface and the business features supported. For the system builder, there must be a version that addresses his particular biases—the application structure, hardware/software architecture, data structures and relationships, and telecommunications architecture.

Conclusion

This discussion has defined a framework for understanding the concept of information systems architecture. The thesis is that it has been the missing link both in the development of an information systems long-range plan and in the linkage of that plan to business goals/objectives and enterprise design. Just as the architect designing a street, building, or city would not think of beginning construction without a blueprint, the information systems executive should not think about implementing a major new application without determining its relation to the total design.

Architecture has been defined as a fit between form and context. A framework was developed for looking first at context and then at form in the quest to integrate the two. This is not an easy job; in fact, the difficulty of establishing a meaningful systems architecture is exactly why more companies have not tackled it. The task takes time and resources, the right people, and a long-term senior management commitment. However, having an architecture is essential because information technology can now provide major strategic advantages for companies. With so much at stake, management must not only understand the concept of information systems architecture but also demand an architecture that can grow and expand with the enterprise.

References

1. Sullivan, Cornelius H. "Rethinking Computer Systems Architecture." *Computerworld Extra*, November 1982.
2. Anthony, Robert N. "Planning and Control Systems: A Framework for Analysis." Division of Research, Harvard University, Boston, MA. 1965.
3. *Cuandra*. Cuandra Associates Inc. Quarterly Index of Online Data Bases. Santa Monica, CA.

9. Managing Risk in Application Development

"Buy no system before its time."

Essay 7 described a technique for prioritizing information systems applications based on the Critical Success Factor planning approach. One of the principal prioritizing criterion reviewed was the degree of risk during the implementation process. Management should have an awareness of the risk involved in a major application and ensure that the proper procedures are in place to manage the risk.

All applications needn't be treated in the same manner. An *ad hoc* financial model or a series of control reports requested by management can probably be handled in a routine way without major risk assessment or project management. However, major production applications such as new production scheduling systems or sales forecasting and order processing systems require careful, professional evaluation and assessment. This is where the risk assessment technique to be described can be of major benefit.

There are compelling reasons for assessing the risks in projects. First, an assessment helps you better understand the project being implemented. An overall idea of its scope and size, its interaction with other projects, and its importance to the company can be better ascertained. Risk assessment helps you compare one project to another, enabling the ranking of projects on a risk scale. This is an important factor in deciding to move ahead on a project. Most business-oriented managers opt for a balanced "portfolio of risks"; that is, they will undertake a high-risk, high-payoff project if they have several lower-risk projects that will come to fruition while they are working on the high-risk one. The balanced-portfolio concept sustains management support and tempers the potential of failure of the high-risk project. Probably the most important reason for risk assessment is that it facilitates more efficient management of projects and assignment of personnel. A high-risk project demands different resources and techniques from the low-risk projects. For example, it would seem prudent to assign your best project manager to the high-risk project. If the high risk is caused by technical considerations, that person should have a good understanding of the project's technical dimension. Stricter control and higher management visibility would be given the high-risk project, with comprehensive reviews and audits scheduled at selected intervals. On the other hand, the low-risk projects can be assigned and managed routinely.

■

Risk Assessment

Professor Warren McFarlan of the Harvard Business School has described a straightforward, easy-to-understand, effective technique for assessing the degree of risk in projects that may be undertaken by a company. This technique has been successfully used by many companies and is fully described in a case study called "The Dallas Tire Corporation"[1] (fictitious name for a real company). This technique can be used to assess risks over a range of projects that affect the IS department. The use illustrated here is in application development, an area where the major part of the IS budget is expended.

The risk-assessment technique utilized divides projects by three risk categories: (1) size, (2) structure, and (3) technology. In the size category, a project is analyzed in terms of projected man-years, dollar costs, elapsed time, and other indicators that measure its overall scope. The longer the time span, the more likely that the business environment will change during the project's life and compound the timing problem. Projects that have a longer time span and require more man-years are higher risk than shorter projects.

A high-structure project is one for which the company has the required expertise—one that has been done before, is familiar to the company, and is straightforward with few if any design options. A low-structure project is one that requires substantial judgment and perspective, presents many options, and calls for considerable flexibility.

The technology risk is related to the company's technological experience and expertise. While a particular technology may be proven in the industry, it is high-risk if it has not yet been applied by the particular company. Projects involving several new hardware devices, such as graphic terminals or a new type of disk storage, warrant high technology risk. When new software is *also* required, the risk can be compounded. The users' knowledge and experience, though not normally considered in the technology-risk category, should be included in the assessment.

The next step is to develop a list of weighted questions in each risk category. The selection and the comparative weighting of these questions are subjective elements, but subjectivity eventually becomes a factor in any technique of this type. The real benefit is to force a critical definition and assessment of risk, and to measure all projects with this same yardstick. Consistency of analysis is one of the key attributes of a tool such as risk assessment.

Figure 1 lists sample questions used in the Dallas Tire Company case. Questions were selected from each of the three risk categories. Each question has a weight, as do the various answers. The question weight is multiplied by the answer weight to obtain the score. Thus, in the size-risk category, if the total systems and programming man-hours were projected to be over 30,000, the score would be 20.

Figure 1
Sample
Questions for
Risk Assessment

A. *Questionnaire Scoring Sheet—Size*

	Answer Weight	Score
1. Total systems and programming man-hours [5 points]		
( ) 100 to 3,000	1	
( ) 3,000 to 15,000	2	
( ) 15,000 to 30,000	3	
( ) Over 30,000	4	
2. What is the estimate in calendar time? [4 points]		_____
( ) 12 months or less	1	
( ) 13 months to 24 months	2	
( ) Over 24 months	3	
3. Length of economic payback [2 points]		_____
( ) Less than 12 months	1	
( ) 12 to 24 months	2	
( ) Over 24 months	3	
4. By whom will the work be performed? [2 points]		_____
( ) Mostly by onsite personnel (IS and/or outside)	1	
( ) Significant portions by onsite and offsite personnel	2	
( ) Mostly by offsite personnel (IS and/or outside)	3	

	Answer Weight	Score
5. Number of departments (other than IS) involved with the system [4 points]		
( ) One	1	
( ) Two	2	
( ) Three or more	3	

6. With how many existing IS systems must the new system interface? [3 points]

( ) None	1	
( ) One	1	
( ) Two	2	
( ) More than two	3	

B. *Questionnaire Scoring Sheet—Structure*

1. The system may best be described as [5 points]

( ) Totally new system	3	
( ) Replacement of an existing manual system	2	
( ) Replacement of an existing automated system	1	

2. If a replacement system is proposed, what percent of existing functions is replaced on a one-to-one basis? [1 point]

( ) 0-25	3	
( ) 25-50	2	
( ) 50-100	1	

3. What is the severity of procedural changes by the proposed system? [5 points]

( ) Low	1	
( ) Medium	2	
( ) High	3	

	Answer *Weight*	<u>*Score*</u>

4. Proposed methods and/or procedures [2 points]

( ) First of kind for data processing   3

( ) First of kind for user   3

( ) Breakthrough required for user acceptance   3

( ) Breakthrough required for data processing

     implementation   3

( ) None of the above   0

5. What degree of flexibility and judgment can be exercised by the system's architect in the area of systems outputs? [1 point]   _____

( ) 0 to 33%   Very little   1

( ) 34 to 66%   Average   2

( ) 67 to 100%   Very high   3

6. How committed is upper-level user management to the system? [5 points]   _____

( ) Somewhat reluctant or unknown   3

( ) Adequate   2

( ) Extremely enthusiastic   1

C. Questionnaire Scoring Sheet – Technology

1. Additional hardware required [1 point]   _____

( ) None   0

( ) CPU   1

( ) Peripheral and/or additional storage to mainframe   1

( ) Terminals   2

( ) Mini or micro   3

2. Which of the above hardware is new to
your organization? [3 points]

	Answer Weight	Score
( ) None	0	
( ) CPU	1	
( ) Peripheral and/or additional storage	2	
( ) Terminals	2	
( ) Mini or micro	3	

3. Special nonstandard hardware required [5 points]   _____

( ) None	0	
( ) CPU	3	
( ) Peripheral and/or additional storage	3	
( ) Terminals	3	
( ) Mini or micro	3	

4. What system software (nonoperating system) is new to
the IS project? [5 points]   _____

( ) Programming language	3	
( ) Data base	3	
( ) Data communications	3	
( ) Other—specify	3	

5. How knowledgeable is the user in the area of IS? [5 points]   _____

( ) First exposure	3	
( ) Previous exposure but limited knowledge	2	
( ) High degree of capability	1	

6. How knowledgeable is the IS team in the proposed
application area? [5 points]   _____

( ) Limited	3	
( ) Understands concept but no experience	2	
( ) Has been involved in prior implementation efforts	1	

Figure 2 illustrates a risk assessment for two projects, coded project X and project Y. The "range" is the minimum and maximum score for the total questions used in each risk category. The percentile for each risk category is derived in the following way:

1. Subtract the low value of the range from the category value.

2. Subtract the low value of the range from the high value of the range.

3. Divide the value in step 1 by the value in step 2.

In this example, project X is a low-risk project, scoring low in all three risk categories; Y appears to be medium risk (falls in the 50th percentile) but is high risk compared to X because of high size and structure risk. The crucial point is that this approach allows you to measure project X against project Y, and, if you decide to implement either or both, it points out the type of project management that should be employed.

Figure 2
Risk Assessment of
Two Projects

Category	Range	Project X		Project Y	
		Category Value	Percentile	Category Value	Percentile
Size	26-83	33	12	72	81
Structure	21-158	39	13	92	52
Technology	21-258	45	10	65	18
Average Percentile			12		50

Project X can be managed routinely, and does not require any special expertise or project management techniques. On the other hand, Y must be watched.

It is relatively low in the technological risk category, so no special expertise is required, but because of its sheer size, a formal project management technique is necessary. Also it may prove desirable to break Y into smaller management-sized units which are assigned and monitored accordingly.

Risk Assessment Application

Project Risk Assessment should be performed at various stages of each project:

- Pre-feasibility stage
- Detailed analysis and design
- Project initiation
- Implementation
- General analysis and design

At the pre-feasibility stage, evaluation may have to be done essentially by "gut feel." Nevertheless, it is important to follow the procedure because it may reveal steps that could be taken to avoid risk. At each successive stage, steps should be adjusted according to the level of risk revealed by the Risk Assessment.

As the implementation proceeds, risk values should decrease, which indicates that the system is progressing properly. An increase in risk potential is a danger signal; higher level management should be informed if an exception condition develops.

If the risk rises considerably, the following additional questions should be asked:

- Are other projects dependent on this project?

- Does this project have sufficient benefits to justify continued development?

- Can this project be eliminated without unduly degrading the system?

- If the project fails, is the company severely hurt?

- Have all the alternatives been considered?

These questions may lead to a decision to discontinue the project or to change certain elements to reduce the risks.

Techniques for Managing Risk

Figure 3 is a two-dimensional matrix using the risk assessment elements of structure and technology. For ease of discussion, size is not shown since it is the least significant to the analysis. There is not much one can do about the size, except to break a large project into smaller units.

90

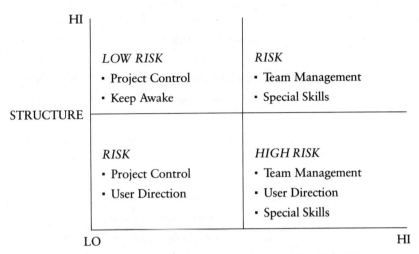

Figure 3
A Two-Dimensional
Matrix for Risk
Assessment

HI

STRUCTURE

LOW RISK
- Project Control
- Keep Awake

RISK
- Team Management
- Special Skills

RISK
- Project Control
- User Direction

HIGH RISK
- Team Management
- User Direction
- Special Skills

LO   HI

COMPANY-RELATIVE TECHNOLOGY

When the degree of technology being employed is low and the project is highly structured and well-understood (high), the project is low risk (upper left quadrant). A simple project control technique can suffice here with the only real risk that the project be ignored and "fall in the cracks." If one stays awake and follows the project, it should most certainly be delivered on time and within budget.

The other extreme is the high-technology, low-structured project (lower right quadrant). These projects can create an experimental, R&D environment. The beginning space flights would fall into this category and, indeed, there were early failures and huge budget overruns. In the information systems application area, installing a nation-wide, all-digital voice and text image electronic mail system is another example of a high-risk project. The technology is evolving but is still relatively new; both hardware and software standards have not yet emerged.

Projects in this quadrant must have strong team management. There has to be a good deal of communication and feedback by a close-knit group that works as a team and is capable of reacting and changing quickly as conditions dictate. This is not a "head in the sand" type of project. Because the structure of the project is low, strong user involvement and direction is a necessity. This is a good area to produce a prototype or pilot program where a piece of the system is tested by a would-be user or customer prior to investing time to formalize the specification. Finally, because it is cutting-edge technology, people with special technical skills are required on the team.

Sometimes small inter-disciplinary ("skunk works") teams are appropriate for this type of project.

Projects in the lower left quadrant require strong user direction on the project team as this is where the risk lies, but require no special skills because they are low-technology projects. A project for a marketing computer-simulation model would fall into this quadrant. There are many high-performance, high-quality sophisticated modeling systems on the market today with fully tested hardware and software. The risk here is that the ultimate users of the model are dealing with a relatively unstructured marketing environment based on changing economic, political, and social conditions. Heavy user-involvement is necessary in this type of situation to clarify changes that occur over the life cycle of the project.

A project in the upper right quadrant has just the opposite characteristics – the structure is known (high) but the technology is leading edge and therefore high risk. Development of the artificial heart or the use of biochips in lieu of silicon chips as computer memory devices are examples of projects in this area. What the devices must do is well-structured, but the technology to accomplish it is not proven.

■ Conclusions

McFarlan[2] makes the following threefold conclusion in discussing this risk assessment technique:

1. We will continue to experience major disappointments as we push into new fields. Today, however, the dimensions of risk can be identified in advance and a decision made as to whether to proceed. If we proceed, we will sometimes fail.

2. The work of the systems development department, in aggregate, may be thought of as a portfolio. What the appropriate components of that portfolio should be at a particular point in time can be debated. The aggregate risk profile of that portfolio, however, is critical to strategic decisions.

3. Project management in the IS field is complex and multidimensional. Different types of projects require different clusters of management tools if they are to succeed.

People argue that the technique described here is subjective in nature in that key variables are the questions selected, the weight to apply to the questions, and, most important, the judgment in answering the questions. However, the value of the approach is in actually exercising the process. Too often major projects are undertaken with no understanding of the risk involved. This is irresponsible decision-making. The major benefit of this process is not merely to understand risk, but to attempt to manage it. Information systems are becoming increasingly important and many are having a strategic impact on the company; all the more reason to use risk factor analysis.

■

References

1. Professor James I. Cash, "Dallas Tire Corporation Case." Harvard Business School. Copyright 1979 by President and Fellows of Harvard College; distributed by Intercollegiate Clearing House, Soldiers Field Road, Boston, MA 02163.
2. McFarlan, F. Warren. "Portfolio Approach to Information Systems." *Harvard Business Review*, Sept.-Oct. 1981.

10. What's Ahead in Information Systems?

■

"An Industry Facing Insurmountable Opportunities"

Anyone who purports to know the future of a still volatile industry like Information Systems should be considered highly suspect. Predictions of the future may be a bit more accurate now than in the mid-50s when prominent industry leaders were stating that as few as 10 to 15 large computer systems could provide the necessary processing power for business and government; however, any prediction remains highly speculative.

First I'll review the principal environment that Alvin Toffler feels will constitute his "Third Wave."[1] Then I'll present a conceptual framework which divides information system developments into eight categories. Finally, I'll elaborate on the major elements of change for each of the categories.

■

Alvin Toffler's Third Wave

Alvin Toffler, in his provocative book *The Third Wave*, categorizes the development of a society into three waves. During the first wave, the agricultural age from 8000 B.C. to 1700 A.D., the majority of people worked the earth as farmers, living primarily off what they produced while trading or purchasing the few items they didn't produce themselves. The second wave, the industrial age, changed all that. The introduction of different forms of energy and machinery spawned businesses and corporations; the accompanying bureaucracy with its hierarchical management style that still predominates: standardization, specialization, and synchronization; concentration, maximization, and centralization. Order, discipline, and assembly-line mentality are the foundations of the second wave.

The third wave, beginning about 1950, is built around four clusters of industries that Toffler thinks will be the backbone of what he calls the new technosphere:

1. *Electronics and computers (the focus of these essays)*

2. *Space industries*
   Toffler projects that we can accomplish things in space not possible on earth. For example, many high-technology materials require delicate, controlled manipulation, which can be accomplished far better in an environment without gravity. TRW has identified 400 alloys we cannot manufacture on earth because of the force of gravity.

3. *Ocean industries*
   The oceans will become the source of much-needed food, minerals (silver, gold, zinc, copper), and phosphate ores for land-based agriculture. We will have aquavillages under the oceans (to accompany the floating factories in space).

4. *Biological industries*
   Toffler feels this area could be the most important of all. Metal-hungry microbes will mine valuable trace metals from ocean water, and bacteria will be used to turn sunlight into electromechanical energy. Micro-organisms will eliminate the need for oil in plastics, pesticides, paints, and many other products. The cloning of mice and *in vitro* fertilization of humans are actual examples of what may be in store.

The technosphere will be blended with the infosphere (the means of producing and distributing information); both will have profound effects on society. Information in the new infosphere will be targeted to select audiences ("demassified") by local newspapers, regional newscasts, the multiple-channeled cable TV, and personalized computer-based information for business use. Toffler sees a shift away from second-wave temporal rhythms of working a prescribed shift, to a more flexible, individually tailored work pattern and style. The epitome of this trend is the electronic cottage, where, because of home computers and terminal links to a host of private and public data bases, activity can again center on the home as it did in the agricultural age or first wave. The key words describing the third wave are flexibility, diversity, and personalization— with the accent on flexible working hours, individually customized compensation packages, participative management, matrix management, and the like. Figure 1 illustrates the changes brought on by the third wave.

Toffler suggests that second-wave leaders today are like passengers on the Titanic squabbling for deck chairs, a dying order trying to hold onto position and power while the world sinks under it. He also reminds us that our Constitution was promulgated by people whose sole managerial experience consisted of running a farm, yet no corporate president would run a company with an organization first sketched by the quill pen of some 18th-century ancestor. Our institutions were designed in a pre-Marx, pre-Darwin, pre-Freud, and pre-Einstein era, and before the airplane, automobile, factory, computer, nuclear bomb, and birth control pill.

Figure 1
Shift in Third-Wave
Thinking

Second Wave
Group ethic
Centralization
Large scale
Structured
Analysis
Take time

Third Wave
Individual choice
Decentralization
Small scale ("divide and conquer")
Flexible
Synthesis
Real-time

The Elements
that Constitute an
Information System

The information systems industry has been the most prolific of any industry within current recollection. Just consider the number of products and services placed in the public domain over the past 35 years. To categorize the major industry developments I will describe a simple conceptual framework. Then I will present selected developments within those classes which promise to have the most impact on management.

Figure 2, a series of concentric rings, shows the elements necessary for a successful information systems. At the center is technology, which is fundamental to all information systems development. Each added ring builds on those within it.

Technology is a vital component of information systems. An example of technology is the development of VLSI (Very Large Scale Integration), a process which enables the fabrication and integration of logic elements on a silicon die called a chip, as small as a quarter of an inch square. The level of integration varies, but soon VLSI technology will enable the etching of the equivalent of one million transistors on a chip.

Architectural design refers to the way we put together the technology. For example, VLSI is used to produce microprocessors, which, in turn, are used over a vast spectrum of applications—from powering personal computers to controlling input, output, and communications within a large-scale computing complex.

Figure 2
Elements of an
Information System

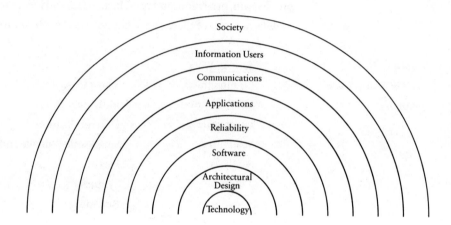

The architectural design of early mainframes placed all the logic of the system into a single central processor, but now complexity has been reduced by separating logical elements into micro-driven subprocessors. The architecture represents the way the system appears to users; an analogy is a prefabricated house where the floors, ceilings, and walls might be made of the same elements, but the way they are put together, the architecture, makes the difference.

Software, the languages and operating systems needed to harness today's computer power, has taken center-stage as the key factor in information systems. Historically, this element has lagged technology and architectural design, though for many years it has been recommended that all three be developed as an entity.

Reliability is often underemphasized, but it is quite important. Reliability, availability, and maintainability are essential ingredients to effective and productive operation of computer systems. An information system, particularly if it's an online one, cannot tolerate downtime and must have 100 percent availability. Reliability is usually achieved by a combination of the technology, design, and software rings.

The *application* is what the computer actually does, be it inventory control, maintaining patients' bills in a hospital, or scheduling school classes.

Communications provide the delivery mechanism for data and information. Data is fed from remote collection points or within the same physical location to a variety of processing and data bases, while information in the form of reports and screen response is sent via computers to the wide range of end users.

The *information users* include the management and non-management end users of the information system within a company.

Society represents the outside environment, covering (1) economic forces such as inflation, competition, and the energy situation; (2) government forces such as laws and taxes, and information demands; and (3) personal forces such as privacy, environment, and individual rights and expectations.

These are the elements that must be present and properly considered to have an effective information system. It is a useful scheme for classifying the myriad of products and services of the information age.

Traditionally, information services has been a technology-driven industry. The planning emphasis has been an inside-out approach when it should be the other way around, from the outside in. The main emphasis should not be whether or not the product will work, but what kind of work it will do; the criterion should not be the ability to do something, but the advisability of doing it; the concentration should be not on how something is done, but on what is done.

Progress has been uneven; obviously there have been some significant, useful achievements made by technologists without outside direction; however, there have been equally significant failures and huge waste of funds working on the wrong problems. The inside-out approach often succeeds the first time, but repeated success does not often occur without a thorough analysis and study of the factors representing the outer rings.

With this framework we can now take a closer look into each of the eight elements described, highlighting these areas that portend the most significant impact on business and government. Figure 3 summarizes the key developments in each category. It is an extensive list, but even so, a review five years from now probably would show fairly serious omissions.

Figure 3
Future IS
Developments

Technology
- VLSI
- Gallium arsenide
- Biochips
- Optical disks
- Point-of-sale optics
- Voice input/output
- Flat-screen display technology and color graphics/image processing

Architectural Design
- Virtual machine extensions
- Microprocessor design
- Distributed data processing
- Firmware extensions
- Data orientation/security
- Parallel processing

Software
- Efficient multirunning
- Enhanced data base management
- Fourth generation languages
- Conversion/expansion emphasis
- Improved quality

Reliability
- Fault logging
- Self-diagnosis
- Replacement in lieu of repair
- Graceful degradation
- Never-fail systems
- Security backup

Applications
- Accelerated saturation
- Strategic systems
- Inter-corporate systems
- Decision-support/expert systems
- CAD/CAM and robotics
- Personal computing

Communications
- Satellites and packet switching
- Fiber optics
- Cellular phones/portable PCs
- "Intelligent" buildings
- Executive workstations

Information Users
- Extensibility
- Senior management users
- Use of portable computers
- Non-computer-professional use

Society
- Cyclical regulation/deregulation
- Security/privacy issue
- Technostress (physical and mental)
- Social usefulness as a criterion

As previously stated, greater densities of electronic elements will be utilized on silicon chips; mass-production techniques will make these chips extremely inexpensive and therefore their use will spread as processors, input/output controllers, memory, and firmware. The successor to silicon chips might be chips made from a compound of gallium and arsenic called gallium arsenide, that promise circuit speeds two to five times greater. In addition, gallium arsenide doesn't overheat and for a given circuit speed consumes only 1/100th of the power required by silicon. A 10-million-instruction-per-second desk-top computer will be available this decade. Some researchers are suggesting that biochips, a semi-living, molecule-size circuit using enzymes and organic proteins, will provide even higher densities and speeds at a later period.

Optical disks, with extremely high density as a result of laser beam technology, will become a mass storage medium. Such disks can store both digital and pictorial data, but once written on, the impression becomes permanent. However, optical disks are well-suited for historical records and will have even wider use once they become erasable.

The grocery front-end checkout counter already utilizes a laser reader to interpret the bars of the universal product code developed by the food industry. Optical readers are being used in retailing and banking operations. These optical/laser readers will cause point-of-sale devices to proliferate. An associated development is the electronic funds transfer system which optically reads a money card or credit card. Debit transactions will also be common.

Keyboards or transaction terminals currently transmit data directly to the computer, which reacts immediately to verify the input and process the particular transaction in real-time. Voice will be used both for input and output with verbal commands recognized by the system, and synthesized voice messages emanating from the system. A voice print can be used to identify a person much as a fingerprint does today.

Flat or plasma screens will replace cathode ray tubes as the principal output device. Plasma screens improve registration and allow graphic and pictorial matter to be displayed. The use of color will be more prevalent in design graphics. And laser printers will be able to produce high-quality printed graphics.

An additional capability will be that of scanning and digitizing images with the ability to alter, change, store, and communicate to remote locations.

Architectural Design

The virtual machine concept will be expanded. Each user will interact with the computer system as if he or she were the only one using it—and this would remain so despite the number of users.

As mentioned, the microprocessor will be utilized for specific functions. The architectural design will follow a divide-and-conquer mode; that is, a job will be "divided" up and each part delegated to a microprocessor. The increased complexity of functions would thus be "conquered." This complexity has been a limiting factor in large-scale systems, affecting both the hardware functions and the software functions built from them.

The firmware-oriented machine is cost-effective and flexible. It affords the opportunity of sub-optimization of languages (e.g., COBOL, FORTRAN, PL/I), operating systems (e.g., UNIX on a chip), the emulation of other machines, and application packages (or at least some portion of them). However, a prerequisite is that the process to be incorporated within the firmware (usually etched chips) be well enough known so that it is not subject to frequent change. Firmware lies somewhere between software and hardware; it is not as flexible and easy to change as software, but is not as permanent as hardware.

Built-in data orientation and security will reduce the unauthorized access to data that now exists, for example, by automatic encryption of proprietary information.

Finally, the parallel processing capabilities that exist in machines such as the Cray X-MT/48 which delivers a peak floating-point processing rate of 1 billion instructions per send (a giga-flop) will provide unheard of speeds. This speed and the use of artificial intelligence are elements in Japan's "fifth-generation" development.

Software

Multirunning, a combination of multiprogramming and multiprocessing, will continue to become more efficient. Operating systems often have more impact on throughput rates and turnaround time than the internal speed of the circuitry. Operating systems will be designed more flexibly and simply, utilizing microprocessor and firmware architectural concepts. By dividing up the functions while embedding many in firmware, efficiency will be greatly improved.

Data base systems will be further enhanced to produce the highly interactive data files required for distributed data processing. They will utilize virtual machine concepts and file structures to economically store huge data files required by the growing number of data base users. The concept of shared files, which are integrated for use locally or in concert with a host system, will be a feature of this generation of data bases.

The key concept in data bases is "relational." Simply stated, relational data bases have files arranged so that the user's view of data (the language he or she uses to access data) is separated from the physical representation of data; one can be changed without altering the other. The goals of relational data base construction are to arrange the files so that the user sub-language is easy to learn, has the ability to readily expand or alter files, and allows the flexibility to access data in formats that were not anticipated at file-development time, in either batch or spontaneous mode.

With the widening circle of computer use as a result of distributed data processing and personal computing, users demand a straightforward simplicity of operation. Computer systems must become friendly, tranquil, and forgiving. Workstations must be operated by non-dedicated users, using simple menu selection and screen tutorial instruction. The user must be able to recover from seemingly out-of-control conditions with the press of a specified function key. Systems must be human-engineered to work for people and not the other way around.

In the past, inquiry languages were "structured," suitable for dedicated administrative users who have learned the language, but not as useful for casual management users who desired system access. The advent of natural-language inquiry which, in the case of a U.S. installation, is the English language, will facilitate a much broader system use. Natural or fourth-generation languages allow non-expert end users to access the company's data base without regard to syntax, grammar, or spelling.

More attention will be given to protecting the user's investment in software, which far outweighs the investment in hardware. Vendors will become more conscious of compatibility and the ability to grow and upgrade without traumatic conversions involving serious interruptions in computer operations. Standardization of data formats, operating systems, and common languages will play a big part in this evolution.

One final comment on software—the need exists to develop better testing and quality methods. It is my opinion that software quality has seriously lagged the improvements in hardware. The future should see the development of improved quality and testing tools, not only to accelerate the development cycle, but to improve the final product.

Reliability

It has become increasingly expensive from a maintenance standpoint to keep communications-oriented systems operable, particularly since many require 24-hour-a-day usage. Because maintenance is a labor-intensive activity, the cost has risen with the rise in wage rates and has not followed the downward curve of electronic circuits, where mass-production techniques have reduced labor requirements dramatically. The key to fifth-generation reliability is ensuring high up-time through the use of fault logging, self-diagnosis, and online test and diagnostics (T&Ds) while controlling costs. T&Ds will become integral parts of the operating system, periodically testing the entire system automatically, checking logs and counters, and printing out or displaying instructions if manual intervention is required; or even fixing the problem automatically. The test routines will cover central processors, peripherals, and workstations as well as the communication lines themselves. Thus the entire computer network will undergo periodic and regular online testing.

In order to control costs, the inexpensive packages and circuits will be replaced rather than repaired. Furthermore, these packages would be replaced, like light bulbs, on a scheduled basis, often in the co-active mode where the user would do the replacing based on simple cookbook-style instructions rather than calling in a maintenance engineer.

The concept of graceful degradation, or fail-soft capability, will become important for future transaction-oriented systems. This means that if a machine failure occurs, backup circuitry can keep the system operational. In certain cases, cost factors will make it more practical to switch off the failing circuit and simulate it via other circuits while the failure is repaired. Even though there might be a system malfunction, the redundant or simulated circuit would take over until the failed unit is fixed or replaced. The system might be slowed for a time, but it would continue to operate, usually without the users noticing any system degradation.

The extension of this type of operation will result in advances in the so called "never-fail" system where redundancy and backup are built-in features. This, along with software and systems approaches, will ensure a high standard of onsite security backup. However, offsite backup will also have to be maintained due to the threat of fire, flood, and other natural disasters.

Applications

There is no question that applications will expand in the years ahead. More and more operational areas in industry and government will be automated. Both vertical saturation (more in-depth automation of existing functions) and horizontal saturation (more automation of heretofore manual or semi-manual application) will occur.

New types of applications will develop. Computers will be used more strategically and will shape rather than merely support a business. (This was explained in Essay 2.) More inter-corporate systems will be developed where computers of two or more separate business enterprises will be linked to give advantage to each.

The use of decision-support systems will be enhanced by the use of expert systems where computer programs can think, reason, develop alternatives, and select the best approach based on the pre-programmed logic of an expert or experts.

Computer-aided design (CAD) and manufacturing (CAM) are already rapidly growing areas of computer applications. Robotics is an extension of CAM. CAM allows computers to control and drive manufacturing processes such as drilling, lathing, and milling. Robotics extends the range of machine-aided functions to die casting and welding, among others.

Many feel that computer-driven robots will mark the next significant stage in the industrial revolution. The Japanese have embraced robotics and currently have more robots than the United States. Sweden, which has always had a penchant for technology, is also among the leading robot producers. Robotics experts feel the next generation of robots will be more sensitive and more intelligent than those in use today, being able, for example, to employ an artificial sense of touch to make decisions based on the texture of an object, and to use a complex vision system to recognize objects based on their shape. Several leading-edge companies are developing what they call "factories of the future" based on advanced robotics.

A final application area of growth is personal computer usage by senior management (explained in Essay 5). The development of true executive-friendly tools will aid this trend.

Communications

The cost of communicating digital data will fall as volume increases and all-digital networks emerge both for local area networks (LANs) and wide area networks. Satellite and packet switching will make data communications more efficient and will support the growth of networking systems. (Packet switching breaks down messages into packets, which are then sent over communication lines.) The technology of packet switching is being developed to provide rapid response time, high reliability, low error rate, dynamic allocation of capacity, and the ability to charge according to traffic volume.

Fiber optics, utilizing glass fibers upon which light beams (from light-emitting diodes or lasers) can travel simultaneously in both directions, will replace copper both in telephone lines and coaxial cable.

A "hot" new industry currently emerging is that of mobile phones or cellular telephony. Projections call for a $10 billion market in 8 to 10 years. The portable terminal is also reaching the point where access to a computer is not limited to a specific facility.

Buildings are also becoming more "intelligent" as they are wired for integrated environmental and security control, tenant accounting and billing, person-to-person and person-to-computer communication, and office automation, all working off a common digital network. There, indeed, will be a connection of areas of business and recreation that were operating as "islands" before.

An executive workstation will emerge that will be truly "user-friendly." It will feature a touch-tone screen, voice input, and an artificial intelligence interface that will make the computer "people literate" rather than force the executive to become "computer literate."

Information Users

"Extensibility," the natural extension of information systems capabilities, will become the order of the day. Information systems are reaching out further and further, from the inner sanctums of the mainframes in the 60's, to remote terminal access in the 70's, to both independent and integrated micro uses in the 80's. Current estimates are that there is one terminal or micro for every three employees in the U.S. This will change to close to a 1-to-1 ratio in the next decade. It is quite likely that some employees will use more than one device during the course of the working day.

Essay 5 indicated that the number of management users will increase. This development will be further accelerated by the entry of new managers who have been trained on computers and consider the executive workstation a natural part of their work milieu.

Computer use will no longer be tied to a physical location; a truly wireless, portable computer will enable the user to communicate from the house, the automobile, the hotel, and, conceivably, while walking or jogging.

Finally, the computer will lure the last professional holdouts—the psychiatrist, philosopher, doctor, lawyer, and those practitioners of the arts and sciences that heretofore have been relatively removed from information systems. Advances in expert systems will make this possible.

Society

Societal issues may prove, in this decade, to be the most vital of all the information system elements. The first major impact is from governmental regulation. IS has become so all-pervasive that it is a direct target for government scrutiny.

IBM, which has held a 60-plus percent share of the computer market almost since its inception, has a history marked by government suits against the company. The most recent one lasted 13 years and was finally dropped with no recommended actions. The government has also instituted commissions to investigate computer applications with broad citizen impact such as electronic funds transfer and the use of the universal product code in grocery stores.

Probably the most significant area is communications. Communications had been a regulated industry, dominated by American Telephone and Telegraph. Then decisions of the Federal Communications Commission required AT&T to spin off its operating companies, but allowed it to enter the information system market on a non-tariff basis to compete with companies in the computer and information systems business. Other deregulation activity has had substantial impact on several industries (transportation, financial, services), and on most industries to some extent.

Individuals have feared the intrusion of the computer, is the form of huge corporate and government data bases, creating a "Big Brother" type of society. The Privacy Act of 1974 provides specific safeguards by requiring federal agencies to permit an individual to examine his or her record, question and contest specific data, and ensure that the data is current and accurate for its intended use. Federal agencies are subject to damages if an individual's rights are violated. This type of legislation will slowly extend to the private sector.

The expanded use of computers will have a significant effect on individuals, who may experience what has been called "technostress," the stress related to coping with new technologies. The primary symptom is anxiety, which can take many forms. However, there can also be physical problems caused by prolonged use of a computer or computer terminal. This can range from wrist and elbow problems to headaches, nausea, and nervous disorders. These types of responses will all have to be faced in the next decade.

The feasibility of computer applications involves three aspects: economic (whether an application is profitable), technological (whether it can be accomplished), and operational (whether it can be effectively installed). An added consideration might be whether it is socially useful and acceptable.

We have the technosphere and infosphere to deliver information to receiving stations on land, on the sea, and in the air. Cellular radio allows us to communicate from our cars; videotex brings instant news, sports, and weather reports to our home and permits our interactive feedback; tele- and video-conferencing beams continuous satellite pictures of meetings between east and west; while portable phones permit us to place a stock order on an airplane. There is a tacit assumption that every citizen wants immediate access to every last bit of information. A question one must ask is whether this information blitz is socially useful. What does it do for the "quality of life?" Citizens, information systems professionals, and managers will all have significant roles to play in dealing with such questions.

A Final Word

This essay has used an analysis of the past, Toffler's first and second waves, to set the stage for the third or information wave. The elements of change in information systems have been reviewed within eight general categories.

Although computers can do wondrous things and can materially aid management in conducting its business, I think we must retain the perspective to realize that the discipline of management still remains part art, part science. There are still things man can do better than machines, and things that only man can do.

There will always be a place for both art and science. I think this point is clearly made in a book called The Analytical Engine, in which the science writer Jeremy Bernstein[2] recalled the career of Charles Babbage, the 19th-century English mathematician who invented the analytical engine that was the forerunner of modern computers. Bernstein mentions the time that Babbage wrote to Lord Tennyson.

"Sir, in your otherwise beautiful poem 'The Vision of Sin' there is a verse which reads

Every moment dies a man

Every moment one is born.

It must be manifest that if this were true, the population of the world would be at a standstill. In truth, the rate of birth is slightly in excess of that of death. I would suggest that in the next edition of your poem you have it read

Every moment dies a man

Every moment $1^{1}/_{16}$ is born...

I am, Sir, yours etc."

May art continue to thrive with science!

References

1. Toffler, Alvin. *The Third Wave*. New York: William Morrow & Company, 1980.
2. "The Assault on Privacy." *Newsweek*, July 27, 1979.